NAVIGATING HR

Simple Tips for People Leaders

Josée Larocque-Patton (JLP)

Suite 300 - 990 Fort St
Victoria, BC, V8V 3K2
Canada

www.friesenpress.com

Thank You to all my family, friends, colleagues and people I have crossed paths with in any format around the world. All of these experiences provided me with material / examples that I could use and learn from to become a better person and stronger leader. I am grateful for any individual or group connection I have made and will continue to make.

ISBN
978-1-5255-4766-9 (Hardcover)
978-1-5255-4767-6 (Paperback)
978-1-5255-4768-3 (eBook)

1. BUSINESS & ECONOMICS, HUMAN RESOURCES & PERSONNEL MANAGEMENT

Distributed to the trade by The Ingram Book Company

CONTENTS

INTRODUCTION

Human Resources is a service department. It does not necessarily make you money, yet proper HR practices can save you a lot of money. The services an organization offers to its employees are things such as recruitment, training and development, fair treatment, employer/employee relations, safe working environment and a variety of other legislative factors. In small- to medium-sized organizations the human resources functions become part of a supervisor, middle manager and even the CEO's responsibilities as the organization does not see a need for an actual HR department or HR functions. Frequent reasons I hear from those types of organizations are: "our organization is not large enough", "we are a family here and work well together", "I have an open door policy and staff can come to me with anything; they don't need HR".

Although these reasons may seem valid, they can be perceived to be "excuses". This does not mean that every organization needs a full HR department, however, organizations that do not employ an HR representative or department become by default HR representatives. The result is that HR duties get spread out between leaders whether you employ one person or a hundred. As a leader in an organization, and for any entrepreneur, it is important to understand your duties as a Human Resources representative.

From the day I started in HR, I loved the profession. Yet what I quickly realized is that I automatically got clumped into a negative perception of what HR is perceived to be: Spies, Hall Monitors, Policy Police, Paper Pushers, Complaints Department, Executioner, Lovey Dovey Department, Camp Counselors, Psychiatrist, Company Watchdog. I kept hearing and reading articles about how HR was not valued as a profession, how HR did not have a seat at the executive table, or at least not as much as it should.

Over my 15-plus years, I have encountered some amazing human resource professionals who you will hear from in this book and others who give the profession a bad reputation. As you know, this is not any different than any other profession. Some people are great at what they do and others are awful. What is important is that you decide what type of entrepreneur, leader, or employee you want to be.

For as long as I can remember, my mother always said I walk to my own beat and create my own path. So why would HR be any different? I did not want to be a typical HR professional clumped into the misconceptions listed above. I want to ensure my focus is on doing what's right and not what is required from me. So how is this possible in a profession that is governed by rules, regulations, policies, and procedures? I am and have always been that person who asks WHY. You know, that person who you talk about at the water cooler, the one who pipes up on a conference call when no one else will, and even that person who other colleagues secretively go to for help/guidance and to be a voice for the team. YEP, that's me. I want to fully understand something before I do it. I want to ensure that I believe in the brand, process, or rule before I enforce it. In HR, I believe it is our job to be objective and truly understand the ins and outs of any situation before making a recommendation, so constantly asking WHY is just the first step to becoming a leader.

This book is meant to provide you with some simple guidance into the world of HR. Just because you are a leader, maybe even an executive, or perhaps newly-promoted does not mean you know how to lead. You became a leader because of certain skills and abilities you have, yet leadership is not for everyone. All leaders have big shoes to fill whether they are leaders with or without a title. Yet, society tends to forget you can be a leader without having a title. You could be a go-to person for questions, a shoulder to cry on or complain to; maybe you're an amazing listener and that is why everyone confides in you. You could also be the leader who has a lot of influence, the person people look up to. Every place of business has a few of you. People who everyone listens to. You influence the culture, people's moods; you are the godmothers or godfathers who people will follow and sometimes slightly fear. The major difference between you and leaders with a title are A: Having a Title and B: Responsibility.

We know so many leaders who have titles who should not be leaders because having a title does not constitute competency. Leaders with a title hold a great deal of responsibility; they are expected to mentor and coach; they are expected to be on their best behaviour 24/7. They are judged, talked about behind their backs, and are typically on stage at all times. What we tend to forget is that we are all human. No one person has the answers to everything, no one person can (usually) run a successful business on their own and once you understand the concepts of Human Resources you will see how important each person is to an organization. Every single employee has a role to play, and it is our duty as leaders to ensure we facilitate the collaboration and cohesiveness of each team member.

—

Proper HR practices can save you a lot of money.

—

The overall goal for HR is to maximize employee contributions to achieve productivity and attain company goals and objectives. When an organization plans their 2-year, 5-year, and 10-year plan, HR should be part of this strategic planning. The general functions for a HR leader can be taken on by any leader as they are mainly to offer advice and create/enforce policies and procedures. For ease of understanding we will divide HR in two main categories. internal and external environmental influences.

Internal Influences:

- This would be your company's culture – the beliefs and values that every employee is to work and live by. Do you have a mission statement, have you had people read and sign off on your company's values?

- What is the structure of your company – how many levels of people are in your organization, how much politics do people have to deal with, what type of bureaucracy exists?

- Engagement – how are people feeling who are part of your company – are they happy, would they recommend you as an employer, do they feel empowered? What is the overall atmosphere you have created?

External Influences:

- The laws of the province, state and country your business operates in will determine a portion of your policies and procedures.

- Economic conditions will influence your labour force, and your company's market conditions.

- Product and service trends and diversity can influence your company.

No matter the type of organization you have, these internal and external influences can affect your business positively and/or negatively.

In this book, we will be examining six main Human Resource topics: recruiting, hiring/onboarding, total rewards, training and development, employee engagement, and finally, performance management. Within each topic you will only be provided with subject matter information that is important to your role as a leader. We are bombarded with *sooo* much nonsense these days that we need to find simpler, faster ways to obtain and share information to increase our efficiency. It's the simple concept of work smarter not harder.

This book is structured in a way for it to be practical and relatable, with information you can use instantly. Any aspiring or current leader can use this material. It is straightforward and cuts out all the nonsense you don't need to know about HR, as I have only given you the things you truly need to know as a leader, business operator, and/or entrepreneur. I will also be sharing tips, successes and horror stories. The horror stories are called "HR Jail" because if you act similarly or run your business similarly there is a very good chance your employees will lodge complaints against you, and you will find yourself with a government infraction. The tips will be identified as "JLP Tips", which mirror a pilot project I started in the summer of 2018 where I provided one tip per day on social media related to HR, leadership, and anything relevant to my viewers and the market. The success and/or other HR-related stories will be identified through the term "Story Time".

RECRUITING

Effective recruiting can make the difference between a business's success or failure. When you are choosing a person or several people to represent your brand you better be damn sure you want this person in your organization. We in HR too often see people being hired because the business needs a body as opposed to waiting until you find the right fit. The notion of having to hire someone because they have a title or skills listed on a resume should not be your main determining factor. You also need to consider a person's attitude, the aura you get from them, the gut feeling you have about how this person will connect with you and others in your organization. I worked and lived on an island for a short while, and believe you me, when someone did not fit within the culture, they got voted off the island. Figuratively, your employees do the same, hence the importance of finding someone who will jive with your culture. One of the first questions you should ask yourself is do you have a culture, what is your company's mission statement. If you want someone to be an ambassador for your brand, you need to have determined what your brand is. Then you can incorporate questions about culture and values into your interview process.

You should not solely hire someone based on intuition as this would be a subjective evaluation process. The ideal recruitment process is a combination of analytical and intuitive decision making. In this chapter, we will get into more details on formulating your interview questions.

———

"Think of recruiting like inviting someone into your home."

———

Think of recruiting like inviting someone into your home. You would not just invite any person into your home, to meet your family and maybe even share a meal with. Hiring employees is the same sort of thing. You are inviting people to your place of work, the place you spend at minimum one-third of your life. Thinking of recruitment strategically, you also want to hire people who have different skills and abilities than you do. If you hire more people like you, it may be fun for a while as you will have things in common, however you will also have the same weaknesses so your company will be missing out on the opportunities to grow and develop in ways you cannot necessarily support.

Before you dive into recruiting at your company there are a few things to consider:

» Are you in a country that requires people to have Government Identification to be employed (e.g. Social Insurance Number, National Identity Card, Permanent Resident card)?

» Are there any laws you are required to follow if employing overseas workers, people with visas, seasonal workers?

» Based on the position, are there age requirements that determine when one may be hired?

» What are the minimum wage legal requirements, rest and break periods, vacation time, as applicable?

» Do you have Equality and Protected Characteristics? These could be protected by your human rights commission and/or a law such as an Equal Pay Act or Employment Equity Act.

» Have you reviewed the legislation and regulations with respect to recruiting people with disabilities? In some parts of the world you must offer workplace accommodation as it's part of an Accessibility for People with Disabilities Act.

» Do you have any bona fide Job Requirements, which would allow you a justifiable reason to discriminate based on role necessity? For example, when hiring firefighters or police officers, there are very specific criteria one needs to have and exams to pass to even be considered for an interview. If you could not pass the medical, or physical ability requirements you would not qualify for a job.

» When can you/must you do a criminal record check?

» Do you have a worker's compensation program? Usually, these are required by law and an employer needs to register and pay fees based on the number of people the company employs.

» Do you have an organizational structure and have you reviewed it to determine who will report to whom?

This list does not include all the things you should consider prior to jumping right into recruiting, yet it should give you an idea of the different things you could be held responsible for.

HR JAIL: I have seen and personally been hired for a role that was not yet developed. In a way, this can be exciting as you are part of something new, and you almost get to write your own job description, yet it can also be less gratifying as you have no target or goals to achieve. Unfortunately, in my experience, I got bored quickly. The employer had a few set projects they knew I wanted to complete, which they assumed would take a year or so to do and I completed within five months. After the five months, I was looking for more work, something I could do as I wanted to make a difference and feel that my skills and knowledge were being used. Instead, I started checking out the Internet for new jobs, got new hobbies as I needed to feel useful. In the end, it turned out to be a great experience, one that set the stage for my career. However, I would not recommend this process as most people prefer to know what they are getting into before signing an offer letter.

So let's get started. Have you defined the role(s) you are seeking to fill? The first step in a recruiting process is:

A. Job Analysis / Job Description

The tasks associated with each role have to be divided into reasonable workloads. This is where a job analysis comes into play. You have to determine the activities and duties you will want someone in the role to perform. You can write a list down with as many things as you can think of, then group the categories together. You want to ensure you are clear and concise yet not repetitive. You also do not want five different positions to be responsible for the same duties. Therefore, if you are writing more than one job description it would be wise to have the drafts for all positions available at the same time.

It is okay for some duties/tasks to cross over from role to role, such as customer service requirements and general soft skills, yet the core duties of each role should be individually defined.

If you were to conduct a formal job analysis such as the method I learned through my HR degree, it would most likely take weeks to complete. A proper job analysis is broken down into parts; most organizations and leaders do not have the time to do a two-week analysis. Therefore, to help with your research you can do a Google search for the role you are looking to fill. You can also ask friends for their guidance. Job titles and tasks are similar in content around the world, therefore to attract candidates you have to speak in a language the candidates are used to. Once you have done your research, take a combination of everything you believe the role will entail to create your own job description. What you should not do is create your own job description without doing some market research. There is a little bit of homework you should do to ensure you are doing what is right for your company. Determine each component from the platform listed below. It will give you a great start to your analysis and job description.

A few key things to determine and include in your job description are:

» More is not better: job descriptions should not be more than 1 to 1.5 pages in length and usually 350 words or less

» Job Title: People screen jobs because of the title. It is common to stick to already existing job titles and to not get too creative. If you want to be different, ensure the title still represents the role e.g. Front Desk Manager vs. First Impressions Manager

» Position Status: Full Time, Part Time, Contract

- » Reporting Manager Title: Director, First Impressions
- » Position Overview: High level 3–5 sentences of what the role entails
- » Primary Responsibilities: These are your tasks and activities
- » General Information: Overall physical demands. Does the employee need to lift a certain amount, stand and not sit? Is evening, weekend, holiday, or shift work involved?
- » Disclaimer: "Employee must perform any and all other related duties as assigned by a supervisor." (This disclaimer is important as there are always other related duties an employee will be asked to do or tasks added on as the company and market develop.)

B. Creating a Job Ad

Your job posting will primarily be the same as your job description with a few listed differences.

- » Introduction of what you are seeking: 2–3 lines – "We are looking for an experienced First Impressions Manager for our Sydney Australia location"
- » Description of your company: 5–8 lines describing who you are, what is your culture
- » Relevant Experience and Qualifications: KSA's – knowledge, skills and abilities – you will be looking for to fill the role including education and/or certifications. Remember to elaborate on this information as this is where an applicant can assess if they meet the basic needs for the role.
- » Compensation and Benefits: Wage or salary range if you want or if you are legally required, company discount information, health and dental benefits, pension plans, bonus possibility. This is

usually high level information explaining you have such benefits yet no numbers are attached. (Be careful on what you advertise unless you are legally required to as you do not want to show competitors your proprietary compensation details.)

» General Information: In addition to what is in the job description include – environment information, employee travel info, relocation requirements or assistance.

» How to Apply: Usually at the bottom of the posting you will have a paragraph that explains to candidates how to apply. Plus, it is always recommended to include something such as: "We thank all applicants for their interest, however only those candidates selected for interviews will be contacted." That way, you are not required to get back to every single applicant. It would be nice if you can do this, but most employers do not have time.

» Legal Disclaimers: If you have any requirements that you need to include this is the time to do so. HR disclaimers need to be included in some print format prior to speaking to candidates. For example, "Only applicants with valid social insurance numbers will be considered", or any other legal requirements such as "You will provide workplace accommodation to a job applicant with a disability during the recruitment, assessment and selection process".

Next, you have to think about where you will advertise and what your budget is, if any.

» Do you have a company website?

» Are you part of any local business group sites?

» Do you have any bulletin boards or local colleges you can post on?

» Coffee shop bulletin boards.

» Local job bank.

» Free classified ads in newspapers and on-line.

» What about LinkedIn? You can use their pay per click job search engine, or post on your own LinkedIn profile.

» Other local community centers or sites that are cost efficient.

» Do you have any referrals from fellow business owners?

» Facebook and Twitter are not usual places to post jobs. However, you can let people know you are looking and refer them to an official job posting.

» There are also many free sites available around the world. In North America, you have www.indeed.com

» Assuming you are a small to medium-sized business, you may not have many employees. If you do, keep in mind you should always post internally if the role you are looking to fill could be a lateral or even promotion for someone internally.

You should also keep in mind the type of applicants you want to attract. If you solely post on bulletin boards at colleges and coffee shops you will only attract people who frequent those locations. If your role is more professional in nature you may want to consider not only your company site but a paid site such as LinkedIn. Job postings are usually up for a minimum of two weeks at a time and up to 30 days at a time. You can expect to get anywhere from 150 applicants in two weeks to up to 300 for 30 days. This is an average for middle management positions. For executive positions, you get a lot fewer and executives usually are more careful in applying for something they are truly interested in and qualified for.

<u>HR JAIL:</u> Free or cheap labour is not the way to go. For small to medium-sized businesses it is common to seek help within your own network, at least to "hold you over". Family and friends will frequently not have the same investment as an external employee. It is sad yet very true, people will take advantage, not necessarily on purpose, of the fact that they know the boss. The employee who is a family member or friend may take more time off than others, or come in late, or what I have seen first-hand, delegate tasks they don't like doing to other people. Then the rest of staff don't feel comfortable saying anything because of the connection to the boss.

In some situations I have seen, family members don't talk for months at a time because of a ruined relationship from having worked together. It is also harder to "switch" off from work when you see your fellow colleagues at home and at work.

On the flipside, I have also seen leaders think they can get away with not paying family or friends a full salary, full salary meaning the equivalent of what they would pay someone else who was external. This actually devalues your employee who is your family or friend, places them in an awkward position, and usually will create anxiety within your relationship.

Story Time:

Many, many years ago, a father (Bob) that I worked with hired his son (John). Bob wanted to help John out, give him his first job. John was a very good student, part of many extracurricular activities at school and according to Bob was genuinely a good kid. For the first 4–5 months, John seemed to be a good worker. He took pride in his job, was always available to come in at the last minute. He was willing to help others by switching shifts. Almost overnight, it seemed he started to take advantage of Bob being the head of the department. John came in late, was frequently tired, productivity was going down until eventually there was an investigation being conducted for theft in the department. Employees were losing their cell phones, money out of their wallets, even gum was being taken out of their lockers. I am sure you know where this story is going. Yes, it was John. When I had to break the news to Bob that his son had been stealing for what we knew was about a month, Bob actually yelled at me, did not believe me and accused me of setting up his son. After the initial shock of the information died down, I showed Bob the multiple video clips of John stealing. During the meeting, I was sitting in my office with Bob, showing him video, explaining the situation when John knocked on my door looking for Bob. John had blue hands. We had placed dye in people's lockers and around their wallets, which is not traceable until you add water. John came running trying to find his dad to ask him how to remove this dye. Bob just looked at me and started crying. He was devastated.

JLP TIP: It is not recommend to hire family/friends. You are putting your reputation on the line for someone you can't be sure will have the same work ethic and integrity as you do. So why place yourself in this position? I have witnessed a few situations where family work well together, yet these examples are minimal.

C. Reviewing Resumes and Selection for Interview

In today's world, when someone has held the same role for three years this can be considered loyalty to the company/position. Someone who has been with a company for 15 years or more in the same position could pose some concern. People wonder do they not have the interest or ambition to develop, have they not been given the opportunity to develop, why are they looking now after so many years, were they let go, were they part of a realignment? Answers to these questions do not necessarily mean the applicant is not a good potential, therefore do not allow yourself to get too caught up in this.

Maternity/paternity leaves, people's health and family situations could also create gaps in history, and applicants tend to "extend" their working time on a resume as they don't want to show they have gaps. Or an applicant will include the year and not month in the time frame they worked for a company so they could have started or ended a job anytime during the same year as this helps hide gaps in employment. Do not automatically shy away from a resume because there is a gap in history. It is not uncommon for people to take lengthy periods of time off between jobs. Enjoying life, spending time with your kids or maybe even travelling is important to people too as it should be. If you are interested in an applicant with gaps I suggest to ask more questions in your pre-screening. Focus on topics of continuous employment. (Just ensure you include those same questions to other applicants as well.)

When someone has very little or no work experience, look for extra-curricular activities, volunteer time, or tutoring experience. This can at least help demonstrate a person's character.

Take a peek at education and certificates. The name of the school or organization from where the diploma or certificate was obtained should always be listed. Then google the school or organization to see if it even exists. It is unfortunate, yet people do falsify their education and work experience all the time.

Reading and scanning resumes can take about 15–30 minutes per resume, so you need to get into a routine to help with your process of elimination. On average, 75–80 per cent of resumes you receive are not qualified for your role. This may seem high, however when people need a job they apply to almost anything and do not zero in on requirements, yet skim through them. When receiving resumes things to consider are:

» Legal Requirements: Is there any indication that would lead you to believe the candidate can or cannot legally work within your country? Does the candidate need a visa and are you willing to sponsor that candidate?

» Education: Do you want someone to have a certain education level?

» Years of Service in the Industry: What is the applicant's number of years of experience within the field?

The above-listed items you can determine fairly quickly, which means you are matching up your desired qualifications with the applicant's resume. This allows you to start dividing your pile into Yes/Maybe/No. When considering skills and abilities dive into the content of each role the applicant has listed on their resume to assess if the tasks they have been responsible for will relate to the role you are seeking to fill. Also review one's personal activities: are there hobbies listed, volunteer time, additional courses taken? These are things that can help you paint a picture of the applicant's character.

Do your homework before you consider inviting someone for an interview. Google the person's name; if something is not legitimate it will tend to pop up on the Internet. This can be both positive and negative for job seekers. If you have put something out there, then it's out there. If someone has been charged with a crime and they are of age, then in many countries this is public information. You can also seek out someone's LinkedIn profile, Twitter account, Instagram, etc. Ask yourself, is this the type of person you want representing you?

For an average of 100 resumes you read you should narrow it down to 10–15 whom you may invite for a pre-screening telephone interview.

D. Interview Question Preparation

To ensure you are objective in your recruitment process, you have to have your questions pre-determined and ask every single applicant the same questions. You do not want someone to claim you have discriminated against them based on an interview, thus the importance of planning.

Step 1: Conduct a telephone pre-screening interview

This will usually last 30–45 minutes. Pre-screening saves time, money and reduces your pool of applicants to people who have good potential for the role you are seeking to fill. Give yourself 10–15 minutes in between calls so that you can properly capture all the information from your call. If you wait until after all your interviews or the end of the day to takes notes you will easily get mixed up between applicants. Create a template that you fill out on the computer or on paper that will list your pre-screening interview questions. Suggested items to document and ask are:

» Applicant's Name, Date and Time of Interview, Position Applying For, Interviewer's Name. I also like to add the applicant's telephone number and email address for easy reference if needed.

Question #1: Ask the applicant about their current job, duties, length of service. You will frequently see how people did not listen to the question and start talking about their first job. This could be a result of being nervous, or it can also indicate a lack of listening and attention to detail. I understand being nervous. I have been there. So every person deserves one get out of jail free card. This is where I like to clarify to the applicant that the question was current job and not past

13

history. Depending on how they take that feedback can help you. You are trying to assess their character, listening skills, presentation, and overall etiquette. If they get the hint that they were not listening to the question you asked, then you will see the interview will go one of two ways. A: It will spark a light in their head that they need to pay better attention, or B: The applicant will not resonate with the comment, it will go over their head and well good luck with the rest of your interview as you will most likely not move forward. Chances are you could make yourself some coffee, since the next 30 minutes are going to suck.

Question #2: What do you know about my company? Why do you want to work at XYZ (insert your company name)? You want applicants to have done their research about you and the company. It does not matter if someone is honest and they tell you they have not had the time. If the applicant actually wants a job and wants to work for your company, the applicant should make time!

Question #3: Ask the applicant about their past jobs as they relate to the role they are applying for. The purpose of this is to see what skills and abilities they have gained previously that will apply and be transferrable to the role you have posted. This is a question where you can get some good "meat and potatoes" out of an applicant. Do they start rambling on, repeating everything on their resume or do they pull out their competencies that could be of value to you. Also, many applicants do not even answer accurately and tell the interviewee you will see on my resume XYZ. Well, Mr. Applicant, yes I can read, and I did read your resume hence why you have been invited to this interview. However, Mr. Applicant, if you do not feel that it's necessary to give me more detail about your past history then that is your choice.

Question #4: The most common question and I still recommend it: Why do you feel you are right for this role? You tend to get a repetition of things that have already been said, yet you can also get some good nuggets that influence you into feeling the person may or may not be the right fit. This is where many successful applicants talk about their culture, values, and things they bring to the table that add value.

Story Time:

I once went to an in-person interview not pre-screening and this question was asked. I have always wanted to answer in a specific way and I felt daring, felt like I wanted to see the reaction on people's faces if I answered in a specific way. I cared about the job; it was actually something I was interested in, so I went for it. Two interviewees asked me "Why do you think you would be a right fit for the role?" and I replied, "Why Not?" The look on their faces; I remember it like it was yesterday – ha ha ha! I continued by saying, "You evidently have an interest in me or you would not be wasting your time asking me to come in for an interview. You do not know me, but I know me. The purpose of this interview is to see if we will fit together. So you tell me what type of person you want for this job, and I will tell you if I am that person." Guess what? I got the job! It was an amazing few years of my life.

Question #5: Then you can ask about the logistics of your role. Our business is open from 7:00 a.m. to 10:00 p.m., 7 days a week. Are there any days or times of the week that you would not be available?

Question #6: What is your expected wage for the role? In some countries there is a law where the wage range is required to be part of your job posting. So if this is the case, asking this question can help you see if what you want to pay is aligned with the applicant's expectations. If you are posting for a minimum wage role you can omit this question.

Question # 7: When are you available to start? Most people out of courtesy will provide their current employer with two weeks' notice. There are some companies or roles that require more notice, and it would be listed in someone's offer/contract.

Question #8: Is there anything additional you would like to add to help consider your application? It is hard to sell oneself on a resume and people do omit some great things about themselves. This is another opportunity to allow the applicant to shine. The results of this question could be an extension of if you are a right fit for the role; applicants will also share more information about what they can bring to the table. An interview either on the phone or in person is a game of how well you can sell yourself, so it should be important for an applicant to provide further details about themselves.

Question #9: Do you have any questions for me? There are both pros and cons on this question. Some HR professionals and leaders feel that if an applicant does not ask questions at all it's a bad sign, others feel that it's okay to not have any questions as their questions may have been answered throughout the discussion. What you don't want is an applicant who repeats themselves over and over, or who asks questions about information that is in the job posting. Usual questions are: How much travel will the job entail? Where will the office be located? What type of benefits are offered?

> » Lastly, it's always good to have some sort of rating system. For a pre-screening it can be based on simple things such as communication skills, experience related to the role, presentation, knowledge of your company. Based on how they answered questions you could rate them on a scale of 1–5, 1 being lowest,

5 being highest. This will help you remember and keep track of applicants.

JLP TIP: Create a system to organize yourself. Remember, your Yes / Maybe / No categories are a very simple process to adapt. You could organize people's resumes and prescreening notes into those three folders.

Step 2: The in-person interview

Just as you did with your pre-screening, you would have your questions preset and allot one hour per interview plus some time in between to give you time to spice up your notes and take a breather. The key to in-person interviews is to do them with two leaders; even better if you can have one male and one female leader. I suggest this for a few reasons:

A. It's nice to have someone else's point of view and compare information with.

B. You can share questions one asks while the other writes down the answers.

C. You have two genders in the room to ensure the applicant feels comfortable and you protect yourselves as leaders. (You do not want to be accused of harassment or discrimination in an interview, which has happened before.)

HR JAIL: Two middle managers were planning on conducting an in-person interview for a role they had open. It was one male (Dave) and one female manager (Kate). Something "urgent" came up and Dave had to go deal with it. Kate was left doing interviews herself with applicants. During one interview, Kate was asking the applicant (Phil) the regular questions, which had all been preset. At some point during the interview, Phil told Kate that he had recently had a heart attack and was now looking to get back into the workforce. Kate being a genuine kind person felt bad for Phil, asked him how he was, did his recovery go well, etc. It was what you would assume to be an innocent conversation between two people. The job Phil was applying for had a few physical demands, however nothing too strenuous. Kate proceeded to ask Phil if he would be able to do those tasks based on his recent heart attack. He said yes. The interview ended, and they left each other amicably. Later Kate advised her colleague Dave about all the applicants she had throughout the day and placed them into Yes/Maybe/No piles. Where do you think Phil's application landed? In the No pile.

Phil later sued the company for discrimination stating that he had not been chosen because of a recent heart attack to which he had no physical limitations and would be able to conduct all aspects of the role he applied for. It was Phil's word against Kate's. Kate could only argue that he was placed into the No pile because other people seemed more qualified. The trigger is one of the regular interview questions was about the physical demands of the role. If Kate did not have the heart attack information she would have asked the physical demand question in the same manner to all applicants. "The job requires you to lift xx amount and bend xx amount from time to time. Are you able to do so?" Since Kate did the interview by herself, she was stuck. Kate went into further discussion about the physical limitations with Phil not out of spite yet to ensure Phil's safety on the job. Her kindness and concern for Phil's health was turned around on her. Phil won the case and the company at which he never worked for had to pay him $25,000.

Now that you have determined someone has the skills to do the role they have applied for, let's see if the applicant be can a good fit for your company. DO NOT ask any personal questions that may be considered unlawful in your country. Should an applicant share personal information, advise the applicant you do not require the information for the interview and continue. Remember the story with Kate and Phil. I can't guarantee that Kate's company would not have been sued, however there is a good chance the situation would have had a different turnout had there been two managers in the interview and had Kate or Dave advised Phil they did not require his medical history for the interview and not engage in open conversation about his recent heart attack.

Story Time:

When I was considering moving back home after having travelled for so long I was on the hunt for a job. Applying to jobs is a full-time job, tailoring your resume, filling out company questionnaires. It is actually one of the parts I dislike most. This particular time in my life I must have applied for about 25–40 jobs. I was open to something more junior yet preferred something within my field to use my skills. Just like other people who share these stories when it rains it pours. I was getting call-backs from so many companies at the same time, being invited in for interviews at the same time. One particular interview I was invited to I was thrilled about. I bought a new dress since I did not have many business clothes in my closet, put on some makeup, which I do not usually wear and walked to the company. It was no more than 15 minutes from my house. It was amazing. I loved the idea that I could walk to and from work every day. As I sat in the waiting room, nervous, you know that feeling of butterflies in your stomach because I was thinking how great it would be to work here. Then came time for my interview. Two women were doing the interview. They proceeded to ask me questions, one after another about my travels, places I have been, food I ate, things I saw. They were having a good old time, laughing, grinning. I had included information in my cover letter about my travelling, the number of countries, experiences and explained how I was looking to get back into the workforce since I had only recently done contract work here and there.

It suddenly dawned on me that for the last 20 minutes they had asked me nothing about my abilities, knowledge or experience, nor were any questions related to the actual job I was applying for. I stopped the ladies in the interview and asked them if they were going to talk about anything related to the job. They stuttered a bit, most likely because I caught them off guard. I felt like I was in the front row of a circus being made fun of and ridiculed at the expense of others. They may have actually just genuinely been interested in what I had done, however it did not feel that way. They never had any intention to actually consider me for the job, yet I was a fun interview to conduct. It made me feel like crap.

I ended up leaving mid-interview and sending a complaint letter to the CEO of the organization. It took a long time yet I did get a response. The CEO as very apologetic, invited me back for an interview with him and the department Vice President. I declined in writing explaining that the role required me to work with those two ladies who interviewed me as one of them would have been a peer and the other my direct manager, therefore it was not a company that I wanted to be part of. Based on the experience they had put me through I was glad I got closure from this.

The more I spoke to my family and friends about this horrific interview, the more I heard other people's stories that were not far off from mine. It was far too common for people to have bad experiences in an interview. This is what got me thinking, *who are these people who call themselves leaders?*

When you are ready to conduct an in-person interview, the following are things you should consider documenting/asking.

» Applicant's Name, Date and Time of Interview, Position Applied For, Interviewer's Name(s). Add the applicant's telephone number and email address if you don't already have them.

» Tell me about yourself. You are looking for their demeanor and attitude.

» What are your greatest strengths and opportunities? How self-aware is the candidate? Is there a weakness that they are too hard on themselves, or work too hard, blah blah blah? I am sure you have heard this response before. None of us are perfect and being self-aware of our shortcomings is important. Everybody has opportunities. It's the point of knowing what they are and doing what you can to work on and improve them.

» Where do you see yourself in five years? This is to demonstrate their ambitions, goals.

» What would your colleagues say about you? Pay attention to the look on their face. If they are hesitant it will show. We all know what people will say about us, it's whether we want to share that or not that is the determining factor.

» Tell me about a time when …? This is where you want to assess their leadership skills, how well they work with others, etc.

» Why did you or are you interested in leaving your current job? You are looking for good or bad reasons for having left or wanting to leave. Also, not everyone is a right fit for a company, so even if they are deciding to leave because they didn't get along with someone or it was not for them, this should not solely influence your decision. See how the applicant speaks about the company. Is it positive or negative?

HR JAIL: I once had an applicant tell me she left her old job because her boss was an asshole, he micromanaged her, didn't let her do her job, etc. Her rant when on for about 17 minutes. I sat there quietly with a smile on my face. When she was done she looked at me. She said, "Oh, I probably should not have gone into that much detail." I replied, "That is your choice." She asked if we would continue the interview. I said. "Should we?" Then she got up and left.

» Why should we hire you? This is similar to the pre-screening question of why do you think you are a right fit for the role, yet I still recommend to ask it again in a different format. Compare notes – is the reason they gave you previously the same as for the in-person interview? You felt they could bring value as they passed the pre-screening so there is no harm in validating your feeling again.

» Give the applicant an opportunity for Q&As. This is also where you should cover bonus, pension, benefits, and status information. By status I mean what is your company's definition of full-time work – is it 40 hours a week or 32 hours a week? If it's a contract job, explain the length of contract, what amenities they will receive or not receive. Even though some of this information would have been in your job posting ad, you want to ensure the applicant is aware and still agrees to the terms.

» Then you should have a post-interview rating system that both leaders fill out individually and then discuss to compare, come to agreement, etc. The rating system can be similar to the pre-screening, however here I'd recommend including more areas to rate, e.g. Adaptability, Maturity, Emotional stability, Leadership potential, Presentation, Ability to work with others, Realistic expectations, etc.

HR JAIL: 'Similar to Me' or 'Similarity-Attraction Bias' is a term that has been researched in depth. It happens not only during an interview process but also in general areas of a workplace. It is a cause of bias when judging people. For example: If during an interview an applicant sees a picture of your dog on your desk and says "You like Daschunds, I love Daschunds. I have a mini short-haired Daschund named Charlie". Automatically, the interviewer will get the warm and fuzzies for the applicant, maybe even their arm hairs will stick up. WHY? Because that applicant is similar to me, meaning similar to you the interviewer. You the interviewer will remember that applicant in a different way than others and subconsciously rate them higher and maybe even hire them. It also happens in many other areas of the workplace such as who you choose to do projects with, or how you rate your employee's performance, etc. According to the research, just being aware of similarity-attraction bias can help you avoid it.

JLP TIP:
- Always advise applicants they will be contacted should they be considered or move to the next level to not leave them hanging.
- Hire for Attitude, Train for Skill.
- Always do interviews with two managers to avoid bias.
- Pay attention to eye movements, body gestures, and position of someone's feet during an in-person interview. Experts who read body language will tell you if their feet are pointing to the door, the person is anxious and wants to leave. If the person is looking up and to the right they are trying to visualize a memory, yet to the left is a constructed memory hence there is a potential it is a lie. There are many factors that play into these tips and I can't guarantee they are foolproof, yet I have used these and many other body language reading tips, and they have validated my gut feeling.

E. Background, Medical and Reference Checks

The purpose of a background/reference check is to seek out if there are any skeletons in the closet. Just like you googled the person when you reviewed their resume, it does not hurt to do another social media check. There is a difference between a background check and a reference check. Not all companies can do background checks, these usually cost $10–15 and you get them from your local police station. The potential employer should be kind and have a system in place and reimburse the applicant for this check even if the applicant does not end up moving forward. You should also check local regulations; employers may be required to pay if they are asking for it. These sort of checks allow the potential employer to ensure an applicant has no criminal record. If you want this to be part of your process, you must advertise this to applicants on your job posting so that people know a condition of employment is to pass a criminal background check. Background checks are becoming more frequent, especially when working with children, government agencies, banks, security firms, and/or information sensitive companies.

Requesting a medical check is similar to a background check. Should acceptance for employment be on a condition to pass a medical examination this has to be very clear at the onset of the application. The costs for medical examinations can be upwards of $500 and therefore the potential employer should be paying for these checks to take place. Medical checks are common for jobs where one's physical/medical condition is important, such as commercial pilots, the military, and law enforcement. It is also very common when working for a global company when living overseas.

Most organizations conduct basic reference checks. The norm is to request applicants to provide 2–3 people who can be references. Those references tend to be positive in nature, although there are people still out there who provide the name of an old boss even if they didn't leave on good terms, or a name of a person who does not even know they have been asked to be a reference. What happens when you call a company and you are told, "We do not provide references and only confirm employment" your number one question to ask is "would you rehire". If you cannot get a straight answer from the person providing a reference, or if the answer is long-winded, beating around the bush it is usually a sign something is up. Think about it … when an employee is great, you can hear it in someone's voice, and the leader will usually automatically have positive things to say.

"When you are checking references do your homework."

HR JAIL: In some countries, there are laws that state a former employer can be liable for hindering someone from receiving an offer from another employer. This means you should tread lightly on giving negative references. If you have nothing nice to say, then don't say it. If you stick with "No Comment", the person checking for the reference should get the hint.

When you are checking references do your homework. Check to ensure the phone number you received is not someone's home. This can be hard to tell nowadays with people only having cell phones and no land lines. All legal business numbers are public so you can find the phone numbers on-line, or Yellow Pages if you still use those. It is unfortunately too frequent where people will give a family member or friend's name to be a reference. These are not recommended as valid reference checks.

Story Time:

I was working in a small division for a larger company for a while and was responsible for all HR functions. Our applicant pool was poor due to the location so you had to be creative and expand your horizons a little. I was seeking to fill a housekeeping role, which did not require much experience yet someone willing to work, be on time, etc. One particular applicant had a very odd resume: things did not match up, there were spelling mistakes. Usually, I would place those in the No pile, however I needed to not follow the process I was used to and think outside the box. So I interviewed the gentleman, he did well, showed interest, and I wanted to give him the benefit of the doubt even though there was something weird I could not pinpoint. When it came time for a reference, I asked for the usual 2–3 names from previous employers with phone numbers, etc. I called the first reference. Everything went smoothly. I called the second reference, and the situation revealed itself.

As I was talking to the person who I thought was a reference, a lady picked up the phone as she wanted to use the phone to make a call. It was the applicant's mother, words were exchanged on the phone as the person who I thought was a reference was indeed the applicant. The mother and applicant argued a bit, then the mother blurted out, "Did you tell this lady you don't know how to read? Maybe she should know this before she hires you." The mother hung up, the gentleman was quiet; I was quiet. At first, I was not sure what to say. It must have felt like a really long 2–3 seconds. The applicant apologized, explained that he lied, he had no references as he got fired from his last jobs when employers found out he could not read. I said to the gentleman, "Ron, you only need to know how to read some basic things for this job, and I would be happy to teach you. Ron accepted my offer and still works at the same location as one of their most reliable employees for over 12 years. Last I heard, he is now a supervisor.

Yes, I still recommend conducting reference checks, however there are so many things that can go wrong with a reference that you also need to have a combination of intuition and having conducted your own homework on the applicant.

Recruitment Takeaways

- ✓ Plan ahead: Who will do the recruiting, what is your budget, how many hours a day you will devote to the process
- ✓ Review your legislation and regulations
- ✓ Know what you're looking for: type of applicant, job requirements
- ✓ Pre-screen with a telephone interview
- ✓ Two people for an in-person interview
- ✓ Do your homework about the applicant

HIRING / ONBOARDING

Now you are excited, maybe even relieved you have narrowed down your pool of applicants and will be choosing someone you feel will be a right fit for your business, and you want them to have started last week. It is almost as if a weight has been lifted from your shoulders when you know you went through this lengthy recruitment process and someone else believes in your company, your brand. Do not get too relieved. There is still much work to do, which you need to be part of. Your next task is to create and provide them with the offer letter.

You also need to have determined what does full-time (FT) work and part-time (PT) work mean to your company. Remember, this would have been discussed during the in-person interview. This is important to reiterate as people need to know before they accept a job offer. Also, if you offer jobs on a contract basis, how long are those contracts, do you offer the same amenities to a contract employee as you do a FT or PT employee? In many companies, a contract person would not be eligible for benefits as they are not there long enough to justify the cost.

There are many different formats of offer letters. I tend to recommend the simplest possible.

» Date/year

» Your company name, address

» The employee's name, address

» A few lines welcoming the person to your company, advising them the date they will start.

» Their title, status (FT, PT or contract), reporting manager's name

» Wage, Vacation Percentage, Bonus, pension plan and benefit information

» The length of your legislative probationary period

» Then you have options for a few different clauses you could include. This is also dependent of the level of position you are hiring for, also the laws and regulations you are required to follow based on your country and state/province.

   - You could include the process/rules around ending employment. How someone needs to provide you with two weeks' notice in writing

   - For more senior positions, you could include termination package information so that a person knows how much they will get paid should they be terminated for any reason that is not a "just cause" reason, e.g. theft, fraud, willful misconduct

- For mid to lower level positions, which tend to be hourly, include the expectations of hours of work, open availability during all business hours, rotation of nights and weekends, etc.
- Dependent on the position, there may be a non-compete clause, or no soliciting clause

✓ Lastly, include a line that would be similar to any document an employee will sign. I have read, understood, received a copy and accept all the terms and conditions. Plus the next line if it's a lower level position: I accept to comply with the policies and procedures of (insert company name) and understand they may be altered based on the needs of the business.

✓ Hiring Manager's Name, Date and Signature

Insert Logo

Full Time Offer of Employment

Insert Employee Name
Insert Employee Address
Insert Employee Phone Number

Personal and Confidential

I am pleased to offer you the position of _____ on a full time basis.
Your role will commence on _____.

Your wage rate will be $_____per hour and your vacation accrual will be %_____ of
your earnings.

You will be reporting to _____ who holds the position of _____.

Probationary Period: 3 Months

Ending Employment: Should you wish to end your employment, you may do so by providing your
manager with two (2) week's written working notice. You will be expected to fulfill your scheduled
duties during your provided notice period. Should we choose to end your employment without
cause you will only be entitled to statutory provincial legislative requirements. Your benefits (if
applicable) would only be continued for the minimum time period required by provincial legislation.

Your position is subject to working flexible hours. Schedules may vary depending on the needs of
the business and will include evenings, weekends as required. Schedules will be posted with as
much advance notice as possible and may be subject to change. Schedule changes will be
communicated by your manager.

Any modification to the offer letter must be done in writing and agreed and accepted by both the
employee and the employer.

Welcome to the team,

_____   _____   _____
Manager Name   **Manager's Signature**   **Date**

I have read, understood, and received a copy of this employment contract, and accept all of its
terms and conditions. I accept to comply to all policies and procedures set forth by (insert
company name) and understand that they may be adapted and / or changed based on the
needs of the business.

_____   _____   _____
Employee Name   **Employee Signature**   **Date**

Company Name, Date

New Employee's Name, Date and Signature

Offer letters tend to be emailed nowadays, yet paper is just as good. If you email, ensure you PDF the document so that it cannot be altered. Allow the person about five days to get back to you. This may seem very long, however when someone is applying for jobs, they usually have applied to many jobs at the same time not just your company. It is not uncommon for people to get more than one offer at a time, I've even had five job offers on the table at once. Hopefully, your applicant will accept the offer you have provided, and should they not this is why you have a pool of applicants. It's always good to have 2–3 people make the finalists' list just in case your plans get derailed.

Story Time:

One applicant, we will call him Andrew, had accepted an offer of employment. Therefore, another finalist had to be notified that they were not chosen to move forward. On Andrew's first day, he arrived with his luggage (the job provided room and board). A little tired from his travels, he wanted to see his accommodation. I took him to his room, he looked around, opened up the cupboards, closet, and bathroom and said to me, "This is it?" I replied, "Yes, this is what we talked about." A shared accommodation, which had bunk beds, the size of the room was no more than 100 square feet including the bathroom. Andrew replied, "I thought you were joking!" I said to Andrew, "This is a cruise ship and you are not a guest. We talked about the room and board frequently. I gave you the dimensions and noted you would most likely be on a top bunk for the first part of your contract."

Andrew took his luggage and left, however he did not realize he just could not leave. He would have to go through security, customs, and at customs he was turned around and forced to come back. I knew this would happen yet I let Andrew play this out on his own. When you fly into a country to board a ship to start a contract the cruise company will usually obtain an in-transit visa or paperwork for you to show so that you can meet the ship in an embarkation/debarkation port. Meaning, you are temporarily allowed in a country as long as you are boarding the ship then heading out to sea. Andrew trying to leave with no paperwork, no return flight was legally not allowed. So Andrew was forced to stay. Part of Andrew's contract is that his travel to and from work for his contract would be paid for as long as he fulfilled the length of his contract. Since he did not want to work and wanted to go back home, he was going to have to pay back the cost of his flight and pay for his own flight home. Andrew had to stay on board for a week so the appropriate paperwork could be generated, have money wired to him to pay back his original flight and cover the cost of his return flight. This is a great example of why it is so important to discuss and agree upon the expectations of a role before an offer is being made and accepted.

Situations like mine can happen even when one party believed there was an agreement. Your employees are like your clients. You are there to serve them and keep them happy. Your onboarding process is the time for you to WOW them. Help them realize they made the right decision by accepting your offer. Provide the best experience possible, organize your onboarding in categories and have a schedule made ahead of time, which you can give to your new hire.

What to Prepare

- ✓ Preparation: A few days before the first day send the new hire an email welcoming them to the team, reminding them about the date of their first day, address, what time they should arrive, who they will meet, what they should wear, should they bring a lunch.

✓ Office Preparation: Ensure the new hire's office is clean, they have the tools they will need such as computer, phone, printer, etc. and maybe a welcome card, chocolates or flowers. I once had an employer leave me flowers in my office for my first day to welcome me to the team. WOW what an impression that was. I loved that job and the company. They knew how to treat their employees.

✓ New Hire Paperwork: You should have these pre-printed and ready for the employee's first day:

Offer letter, Confidentiality agreement, Health and Safety agreement, Policies and Procedures agreement, Workplace Harassment and Violence policy, and Employee Handbook are your general documents. There are many more you can add based on your organization's needs and/or legislative requirements. If you have a computer system to create a new employee profile you could prepare it prior to their arrival, however you may not have all the information you need, and there is always a possibility that the employee does not show up. Therefore, I would not suggest creating profiles in your system or even on paper until the first day the employee is with you.

✓ Day 1: Introduction and Personal Items: Meet fellow employees, meet union steward if applicable, other leaders, general new hire paperwork, payday, how union dues work, explain which jobs are unionized and which are not, benefit, discounts, schedules, parking, office or locker, break room, dress code, uniforms, vacation process. The employee is not usually left alone this day – they are with someone for the entire day or shift. They also usually do not work a full day. Day 1 could be conducted by HR personnel or the hiring manager.

✓ Day 2: Safety, Security and Business Information: Tour the company, entrances, exits, fire procedure, first aid information, ID badge, how to report accidents, incidents, health and safety committee, history of the business, size, reporting structure, company values, mission statement, customer service philosophy. Depending on the employee's department there could be sales, merchandising, housekeeping, dining room, and philosophies to review. Review bulletin boards, communication processes, staff meeting, who to go to for help. This is when you would also meet your buddy or coach – the person who will help train you. If you have time, you may spend an hour or a few hours with them otherwise by Day 3 is when you start your on-the-job training.

✓ Day 3: On-the-job training is called OJT: Prior to a peer being the trainer, ensure the peer has been trained on what and how to train. This is called "Train the Trainer". Many companies choose their best employee to train new employees, however just because someone is your best employee does not mean they are your best trainer. Most people forget what they did last week let alone what happened during their first weeks on board. Training someone is not just having them follow you around to see what you do, or being those extra hands to help you get your work done. Create a structure as to what should take place during an onboarding. You can have a general checklist that applies to every new person, then subsequent checklists by department. Each department head would need to create their own checklist to ensure all necessary areas are covered. Thus each department should have at least one "trainer".

✓ Day 4 and 5: Repeat what is from Day 3 on-the-job training. Everyone learns at a different pace and has a personal learning style, so have a variety of visual, auditory and kinesthetic learning opportunities. Remind the employee to be open; if there is something they do not understand/or would like more clarification it is up to them to ask. You will assume no news is good news.

✓ Day 6: Follow-up: This is the time for the leader to spend some time with your new hire to review their first week, discuss what they liked or what they did not like to get a better understanding of what the second week's focus will be. You can even have a formal onboarding evaluation document you ask the new hire to complete. Feedback and open communication is very important. By Day 6, the employee may be ready to do a shift on their own and having their trainer check in every so often. In other locations, there may be more training that is required or a course the new hire must take to obtain a certification. Your path will depend on how much previous experience your new hire has. Have they done a similar role in a different company and now you simply need to "brandify" them or are you starting from scratch? No matter how you choose your structure it's important for the new hire to know exactly what is expected of them and what they are getting into. Even for an executive, do not withhold information because you may be nervous to scare them off. Honesty is the best policy.

✓ Day 7 and beyond: This will depend on each organization and what level of position you hired for. In some positions, onboarding can last up to 90 days. No matter how long your onboarding is, the purpose is to have a calendar and schedule pre-set, allowing for some flexibility as things do not always go as planned.

A few years ago I was an HRBP for a large international company. The site I worked at employed nearly a thousand employees from various countries, making it a diverse and fascinating place to work. With so many different cultures, my team and I always had a strong focus on helping employees understand our culture, values and policies. We educated our leaders on the same, but also on how to lead such a diverse workforce. While it sounds silly to say, I've learnt over the years that everyone, no matter their language, where they are from or the job they did, wants to be valued, appreciated, respected.

While in my office one day I was approached by a team member and informed about how they were treated by their new leader who recently joined the location. What this individual told me was not against the law, but it certainly did not measure up to our expectations of our leaders and how we should value and appreciate our teams. I asked a few more questions and then paid the department head a visit.

During my conversation with the department head, I learnt that the leader transferred from a different location in order to make a fresh start. I also learnt that this leader displayed similar behaviour patterns at their previous location and while there have been some conversations around changing the behaviour, that is where it stopped. I worked with the department head in order to gather feedback from the team. We met with the leader and outlined clear expectations about what performance should look like, checked in on a frequent basis and reviewed the area's sales and service experience reports. We had to help this leader understand how their actions impacted their team and ultimately the quality of the service we provided, as well as that improvements in their behaviour would not only improve team spirit, but ultimately also sales and service.

Over the next couple of months, we were able to help this leader improve and mend the relationship with their team. I am not taking any credit here as the leader did all the work, we only provided the framework to operate in. It could have gone either way though. We were however honest in our feedback and were able to give specific examples on where the leader did not meet our expectations. We also did not judge the individual and made sure they were aware that we wanted them to be successful, hence why we shared this with them.

When we think about engaging our teams, we think about free pizza at work, drinks in the pub or handing out discount shopping vouchers to make the team happy. While these certainly help in the short term, we can only truly engage our teams by making sure they have a great work environment, are cared for, and have a workplace where they are safe and all this starts with onboarding. As HR partners, this requires us to sometimes address difficult situations which may not be the most comfortable. No matter how difficult it may be, we have to be honest. For those who are not leading appropriately and doing right by their teams, it may be because no-one has taking the time to have an open and honest conversation. Something so

*simple as a conversation may just be what they need to turn
things around.*

*To truly show we appreciate, value and respect our teams,
we have to take care of them and provide them with a welcoming work environment. In order to do so, we have to be
honest with ourselves, our leaders and our teams.*

Dewald

15 Years in HR

United Kingdom / South Africa

HR JAIL: I started a new job some years ago, after I had decided to relocate. I bought a condo and wanted to set some roots down in a particular city. I accepted the job about 5–6 weeks before it started. This gave me time to give my current employer notice and get established in my new home. I had been made aware of the reporting structure prior to accepting the offer and my boss was not located in the same town as the job was, which was fine with me as I was used to working remotely and having my direct leader miles away. About two days before my first day, I received an email from my new boss that she would not be able to make it in for my first day yet she had made arrangements for someone to meet me. She would be in contact as to when we would meet face to face.

Like any other new employee on my first day, I put my best suit on, did my hair, and brought my new briefcase to work ready with new pens, highlighters and a few things I would want in my office – just like a first day at school wanting to stock up your locker to make it your own. I arrived at work at our pre-agreed scheduled time and there were lots of people there yet no one to greet me. No one I found seemed to know who I was or why I was there. The person my boss had arranged for me to meet, the general manager was not yet at work. We will call him Brad. Eventually, I was shown to Brad's office and sat in his office waiting for him for close to an hour. Brad had prior commitments that morning and was asked last minute by my boss to be there for me so he asked one of his direct reports to "welcome" me until he got to work. However, I was unaware of that and it seemed no one else was aware so I never came in contact with the person who was meant to welcome me. I remember feeling sick to my stomach, the first few hours. As a new hire, no one knew I was coming, my boss was not there to meet me and the thoughts crossed my mind, "What have I done? I left an amazing job, amazing company because I selfishly wanted to try something new." Me being me, I brushed it off saying to myself, "No, I am making a big deal out of nothing. I am sure this is just an honest mistake."

Brad eventually arrived, and he was lovely. Very apologetic, he introduced me to Dave who was the person meant to welcome me, and he was lovely too. You see, I was making a big deal out of nothing. My first impression of the people I was going to support was amazing. Then I kept meeting more people, colleagues, and others who would be my clients. They were all great. I left my first day feeling happy and relieved. Keep in mind I still had little to no information from my own boss and did not know when I would meet her.

On my second day, I met with Brad to do what I thought was set up my office, get my computer, company phone, etc. After all, this was what I had discussed with my boss. Brad felt bad. He showed me to my office, which had been a storage room. It had not yet been cleaned out, there were still so many boxes and random things in it. He had no idea about a computer or phone. So instead of getting upset, I changed my shoes got some cleaning material and started clearing out and cleaning that storage room. If this was going to be my office, I was going to make it my office. Brad gave me a budget for furniture, stationary, etc. I borrowed my dad's truck, and borrowed my dad, and we went shopping for a desk, filing cabinet, chairs, etc. We put everything in his truck and brought it back to work. On the weekend, I painted the office with my dad and set up the furniture, etc.

So one week later, I now had a beautiful office that I put together with the help of my dad. Brad could not believe what I had done. I remember the look on his face, he laughed and smiled at the same time. He took me out for lunch that day and this began what I thought was going to be a great working relationship. Even though I now had an office, I still had no computer and no cell phone. So I had to use my personal cell phone and bounce around to other colleagues' computers to do online training, answer emails, etc. This lasted for weeks.

I eventually met my boss by mid-second week. She felt bad for not having been there or been prepared. She gave me a binder that I swear was six inches thick. It was all the HR policies, procedures, and company information I needed to know. So until I had a computer and phone I studied and read that book inside out. The majority of the orientation I did with my colleagues was over the phone as everyone was spread out throughout the country. But, I slowly started to get exposed to that original gut feeling I had within my first few hours on the job. Fellow peers talked behind each other's back. A lot. Most did not like the boss and talked behind her back as well. There was a very strong division in the team and as a new person it felt like people were trying to rally me to join their side of the team. I have a very strong personality, and have had since I was a child yet I usually get along with almost anyone. Some people you get along with better than others. Yet, if I truly had an issue with someone I would discuss it face and face.

I had never been exposed to such a toxic environment. I was at a loss. I spoke to my mom as I was so distraught. I remember crying many times thinking, "What have I done? I made the wrong decision and now I'm stuck." My mom told me she once worked in an environment that was toxic as well. She had never told me the story before, and I was saddened to know these things happens more often than we know. The other friends I spoke to also had similar toxic environment stories. So I decided to speak to my boss. I was open, very open and direct as I am. I explained how it was unfortunate that it took so long for her to meet me face to face; she had known for over a month that I was coming. I had no office, no tools to do my job, I was using my personal cell phone for work that finally they were reimbursing me for two months into the job. Then I asked her what was wrong with the team; why did people not like each other? Did she know that many people did not like her and then gave her all these examples of things I had been told by others. I was genuinely asking, as I wanted help with how to make this right. I really like the people I was meant to work with day in and day out, yet the HR team that I was part of was not a team.

She had no idea, or claimed she had no idea what I was talking about. Even though I later found out she did know a lot of what I told her. There had been a big argument some eight months ago at a meeting. The argument was over the division in the team; some people got invited to things while others didn't. It was like high school when some people are part of the cool crowd and others get excluded. I didn't like cliques in high school, and I certainly don't like them as an adult. Now I was the idiot who opened up Pandora's Box. I exposed this toxic team to my boss. I was basically telling my boss she had a toxic team and asking why she was not doing anything about it. All this after having just been there for a few months. She, just like any other human, got defensive and decided to see what I was talking about. She questioned people on the team about the cliques, the info I shared with her and this created a tidal wave. It was one of the worst and best onboarding experiences I have ever had. The writing was on the wall from the beginning, although I kept trying to avoid seeing the signs this was not going to work out.

After even more turmoil of 'he said, she said', I left that company but kept in contact with many of the operations people I worked with for just those few months. I am forever grateful for this experience as I learned a lot about the ugly side of HR, what to say and not to say and vowed I would ensure any new hire I was responsible for would have an amazing onboarding experience.

***

Measurement: Another important part of someone's first few months in a new job is to measure their performance or the lack thereof. These are usually called probationary reviews. Depending on your legislation, you may be required to do a probationary review at 30 days, 90 days or even six months. The law requires you to do it at certain times in case the person is not working out and you want to terminate them. Whether the new hire will pass probation or not, a good rule of thumb is to assess their performance every 30 days. Set your meeting days the first week the employee starts. This will help you guide the person if they are not on the right track and give them a chance to improve. By no means does this mean you should only speak to your new hire once every 30 days. Remember, by the sixth day you should discuss their onboarding and training plan for the upcoming week. Usually checking in with them once a week for the first 60 days can ensure they have the support they need to succeed.

JLP Tip:

- Have a bulletin board or newsletter you circulate to welcome your new hires. Include a small blurb about this new hire, maybe even with a picture so everyone on the team can welcome them.
- Create a structure for your onboarding, with daily checklists so people know ahead of time what they are responsible for.
- Train your trainer, do not just choose your best employee to be the trainer.
- Keep in contact with your new hire so they remember what day they start. I have seen many people forget or not show up so having regular communication can help avoid this.
- Remember that a new hire will not be familiar with your company lingo so be careful in using terms they are not familiar with.
- Do not leave your new hire alone. A new hire is nervous and anxious. They need to feel comfortable in the environment before they can spread their wings.
- Explain the procedures, policies, and ins and outs of the company. Do not solely let them read it in a book, or find out in a training session.
- Follow up: Checking in with your new hire is important to their success and yours. You have invested a lot of time and money already in the recruitment process. You should be doing what you can to ensure they succeed.

Remember! Performance assessments for employees on probation need to be more tailored and frequent than those for regular non-probationary employees.

Hiring and Onboarding Takeaways

- ✓ Have a pool of finalists in case you need a back-up plan
- ✓ First impressions matter, your employee is also a client/customer
- ✓ Create an onboarding schedule
- ✓ Train your trainers

✓ Provide 3–5 days for general onboarding before leaving an employee on their own

✓ Follow up and Check In

✓ Conduct your probationary assessments more frequently than you legislatively need to. Every 30 days for three months can help set your employee up for success.

TOTAL REWARDS

Total rewards is not the membership you sign up for when you are enjoying your vacation in Las Vegas. In the world of HR, total rewards is the pay and incentive package you offer your employees. It is what helps you attract someone to a position and hopefully part of what retains them and keeps them motivated. When you are just starting out, or if you have only a few employees, you may not think of Total Rewards as a necessity to your business. You will most likely find someone to help you fill a need, discuss what you believe you need help with, then touch upon a wage/salary you both agree with and if the person is interested they will start on Monday. That is very common for small- to medium-sized businesses.

Sit back and think logically about this next sentence. Wages cost you 40–70 per cent of your overall business budget. What does this mean to you and your business? If you are investing 40–70 per cent of your money to have someone help you, someone who represents you, why wouldn't you take all steps necessary to ensure you have a Total Rewards program in your business? You do not need to have everything written in stone, yet you should start with a good foundation and build from there. Your Total Rewards system helps shape the performance of your company as it is directly connected to the behaviour and engagement of your employees. Whether you have two employees or a hundred, no one works for free. If you want your company to have goals, you and your team will need to be given metrics to achieve those goals. In turn, those metrics would be tied to your Total Rewards system. If you have an employee who is not performing, or is dishonest, you do not want to reward them the same way as you would other high performers, correct? Money is a driving factor for Total Rewards, yet gratification for achieving goals, recognition, status and general growth and development are almost as important if not more important components of Total Rewards.

That being said, there are two main parts of Total Rewards: Money and Everything Else. The appropriate terms for these are Extrinsic and Intrinsic rewards. As we are focusing on simplicity, we will continue with our two categories of money and everything else. Money will be defined as the wage/salary that an employee is given, plus anything that costs you the employer money such as: vacation percentage, sick time, health and dental benefits, retirement savings plans, pension plans. Everything else will include the challenges someone experiences, variety in tasks, autonomy, trust between employee and employer, positive feedback and recognition from colleagues and leader – things that give people gratification and a sense of purpose, knowing you are making a difference, seeing progress you are making, and the feeling of competency.

These are a few things to consider when you want to create a Total Rewards program for your business. We will go into each section individually: Wages (with bonus), Vacation and Sick Time, Health and Dental, Other, then we will briefly discuss other parts of Total Rewards such as recognition (non-cash bonus employee month)

Wages

Assuming you have done your job analysis when you created your job description you decided what skills and abilities are needed for the different roles you have in your organization now you can move into payment for each of those roles. What are your next steps to determine your employee's financial rewards?

1. Determine Your Wage Structure:
   » Do you have a legal minimum wage you must pay? Ensure you are following your legislation
   » Google the market; what are other roles paying with similar tasks? You want to stay competitive in the market therefore you need to pay within market range
   » What can you afford to pay? If you have the ability to give a little bit more than the market, you could increase your requirements for the role, thus helping you weed out the B players and solely focus on A players during your applicant process. This would mean you have a more stringent hiring process. If you are going to give more you should expect more.

2. Full Time, Part time or Contract:
   Based on what you determined in your recruitment process there is a difference in how you choose to pay someone. Usually, a part-time employee is hourly, where a full-time employee can be hourly

or salaried. A contract employee can also be hourly or salaried. Either method of payment you choose is up to you.

3. Hourly or Salary:

There are advantages and disadvantages to both. You could also choose to do a combination of both throughout your business. Some positions are hourly, while others mid to higher level you choose to make salaried positions.

Hourly Advantage	Hourly Disadvantage	Salary Advantage	Salary Disadvantage
Track: Implement tracking system to record time in/out, break time	Possibility of altering / lying on the tracking system	Trust / honor system with employees Work extra hours without additional compensation	Easier to steal time, when not tracking. Take longer breaks, come in late, leave early
Shift Length: Better control of hours you want people to work; determine start and end shift times, and breaks	Need extra help or someone calls in sick can run you into challenges as most legislation governs the length of a shift and maximum hours per week.	More flexibility with schedule	People working odd shifts, not well balanced, extra-long day, then a short day can lead to people feeling overworked, less work life balance. Also less likely to take breaks
Statutory Holidays: You have more control over who can work a stat, which can help manage a budget	Stat pay costs you more for someone with higher wages, plus there is a possibility of double time pay on a stat holiday	Stat pay is based on legislative eligibility.	People get paid stat pay even if not working, based on legislation

Hourly Advantage	Hourly Disadvantage	Salary Advantage	Salary Disadvantage
Regular Wages: Control wages as you decide who works when	Overtime costs not frequently budgeted for	Less wage cost fluctuation as you automatically know how much people are paid	Some legislation states that if a salary is low, the employee may still be eligible for overtime
Engagement: Work-life separation, thus allowing the employee to refresh between shifts	Employees tend to work their shift and leave, the role is seen more as a job than a career. Mental association with hourly work is that it is low skilled, lower paid jobs	Employees feel more valued, the company has a higher investment in them, can be more of an ambassador to your brand	Employees can have a sense of entitlement
Career Development: When they are interested in career development, usually quite invested as it's a choice with the employer not an expectation	Less interest in making the job a career. Will leave job for higher paying job elsewhere	More opportunities for growth and development, taking part in succession planning	Employees upset when not considered for career development. Employer tends to expect more, therefore expect employees to be on a succession planning path.
Other: Easier to replace, terminate, costs less	When economic downturn, could have hours reduced, thus a pay cut, leading to disengagement	Sense of job security	Termination cost high Expectations of benefits: health and dental, pension plans, sick time paid, etc.

4. <u>Build Your Wage Structure</u>

You should create a wage grid, also frequently called a salary scale. An easy way to start is to decide your mid-range salary/wage for the positions you have. A mid-range is assuming someone has 5–10 years of experience in the role and on average it would take a minimum level employee 5–10 years to go from your minimum wage to your medium wage level assuming a yearly 2% increase. Below are the two common types of scales used.

Model A – Hourly:

Job Title	Minimum Wage	Medium Wage	Maximum Wage
Receptionist	$15.00	$18.00	$21.00
Front Desk Manager	$19.00	$22.00	$25.00
Hotel Director / General Manager	$23.00	$26.00	$29.00

Model A – Salary (based on 37.5 hour work week)

Job Title	Minimum Wage	Medium Wage	Maximum Wage
Receptionist	$29,250	$35,100	$40,950
Front Desk Manager	$37,050	$42,900	$48,750
Hotel Director / General Manager	$44,850	$50,700	$56,550

✓ In Model A, you have about a 20 per cent difference in wages between the minimum to medium, then medium to maximum. I chose 20 per cent as an example for no particular reason.

✓ Common gaps between wages are anywhere from 10 per cent to upwards of 40 per cent, this example of 20 per cent differentiation is just one example.

✓ Model A is frequently called a pay for performance system. Wider gaps between minimum, medium and maximum wages allows the employer more flexibility to choose a wage that suits the employee's skills and abilities.

✓ The better one's performance is, the more opportunity for financial reward.

✓ Gaps between the grids are important for you to differentiate between skill, tenure, and they should be significant enough for you to comfortably recognize competency.

✓ To ensure fairness, no wages should be differentiated by gender, yet as noted above by skill and tenure.

✓ You also do not need one grid for each position. If you have positions of similar level, responsibility, skills and abilities you could include them in the same wage grid.

For example: Receptionist + Housekeeper + Cleaner

Model B – Receptionist Hourly

Pay Grade	Classification	Minimum Wage	Medium Wage	Maximum Wage
Grade 1	0–3 Months	$15.00	$18.00	$21.00

Pay Grade	Classification	Minimum Wage	Medium Wage	Maximum Wage
Grade 2	1–2 years	$15.60	$18.60	$21.60
Grade 3	3–5 years	$16.20	$19.20	$22.20
Grade 4	6–8 years	$17.20	$20.20	$23.20
Grade 5	8–10 years	$18.20	$21.20	$24.20

Model B – Receptionist Salary will be very similar to Model B Hourly; the main difference is you would alter your hourly rates for a salary

As described in Model B, you can include classifications for your wage grid. These classifications can be created in a variety of ways. One of them is by years of service as shown in the example, others could be a point system that demonstrate the more responsibility an employee is given the higher the points they receive meaning the higher possibility of pay they can receive.

———

Include a clause in all employee documentation and in the pay scale that wage increases are "recommendations" and always subject to the performance of an employee who must be in good standing."

———

Classification systems exist in all types of business models, unionized and non-unionized, small, medium and large-sized companies. They are a way to give more specific direction to leaders when deciding wage rates, yet they could also constrain a leader when you have poor performers in your business. If you are going to have a classification type grid there will be expectations by your employees that they are paid according to your company's classification system. This means you may have less flexibility to work within someone's performance since you have specific criteria as to when someone should receive an increase. When someone is not performing, they should not receive a wage increase at all. Otherwise, it is a double standard: "Thank you for not performing this whole year, here is a 35 cent increase." However, with Model B you would be breaking your company policies if you did not pay someone according to your wage grid, therefore you would be "forced" to give someone an increase even if it meant moving them to the minimum of the grid based on their years of service. To avoid being forced to give increases because of your processes, include a clause in all employee documentation and in the pay scale that wage increases are "recommendations" and always subject to the performance of an employee who must be in good standing.

If your minimum wage changes according to legislation, you will need to adjust your wage grid model. Model A will be slightly easier to adapt than Model B only because you have fewer numbers to crunch, still giving you more flexibility.

This is not to say that one method is better than the other. It will depend on your business model, the amount of your labour budget and, how much effort you would like to place on managing your Total Rewards program.

5. Wage Increases

Will you offer an opportunity for employees to obtain a yearly wage increase based on their performance or based on their years of service? If you are unionized, all terms will be stipulated in your collective bargaining agreement. Whichever method you choose, this should also influence the type of wage grid structure you use within your business. If you want more flexibility you will go with Model A, as just described above. The tip to remember here is documentation. If employees will be eligible for an increase based on their performance, they need to know how they are not performing, which means you need to evaluate their performance. This should be documented on a formal performance appraisal form. We will discuss appraisals in more detail in the Performance Management section.

6. Bonus Structure

    Are you going to provide someone with a base wage or will you include other monetary incentives? Many organizations like to have their employees more involved, thus giving them an opportunity to have "skin in the game". Providing an opportunity for an employee to make more than their base wage usually increases their engagement and overall desire to achieve their goals. There are three main bonus structures you can choose from:

    > A: Individual
    > B: Group
    > C: Company

    A: Individual Bonus Structure

    These are metrics pre-set that are solely based on one's own performance and have no bearing on other employees and sometimes are not reflective on the company's performance. If a fellow employee or even if the company does not meet their metric yet the individual does, the individual will still get their bonus. To choose a simple way for this metric it would be percentage based. At the beginning of every year, each employee is given their performance targets for the year, which can be discussed mid-year or preferably once a quarter. The employee's performance is reviewed to see if they are on target to hit their yearly metrics and if they are not the employee is given coaching and mentoring to help them achieve their targets. The process of tracking performance must be formalized and fair for all individuals, thus documented on a performance template. Individual Bonus structures range from 2–4 per cent to upwards of 25–30 per cent of an employee's wage. So, if the Front Desk Manager had a five per cent eligibility bonus on her/his starting salary of $37,050, that individual could obtain $1,852.50 of yearly bonus. You also need to consider that the incentive has to be worthwhile for an employee. It needs to motivate someone and feel like a real financial reward. If the amount is too nominal it will not resonate with someone.

Decide if you are having an all or nothing payout model or a partial payout model. This means if the employee hits a portion of their metrics, they still get a portion of their bonus. This is usually a fair approach to take as opposed to an all or nothing model, meaning you must achieve all metrics to get any of your bonus.

Then you should also divide the tasks and yearly goals into bi-yearly or even quarterly segments. Have employees work towards achieving their metrics in parts. If you do not choose to divide it, then an employee may hit all their targets at the beginning of the year and choose to relax and coast for the remaining part of the year. The opposite can be true as well; an employee may be lazy at the beginning of the year, procrastinate and wait until the end of your fiscal year to start working towards their goals.

Commissions are another form of individual bonus structure. In you are in sales for example, you get a portion of the sales you make. These are great incentives for individual performance as the sky is the limit here. The more money you make for the company, the more money you make for yourself as well.

B: Group Bonus Structure

These metrics are usually based on people who are within your department thus working similar roles to you. Furthermore, this can also be an opportunity to cross-pollinate between departments. Have one or two members from each department work on yearly projects together and rotate the teams so that employees get exposure to others within the company. This could increase cohesiveness within the organization and reduce silos between departments. Other advantages to group bonuses is that they force the team to communicate and collaborate with each other, and for employees to get to know each other when they otherwise may not have made the effort. This also may help increase loyalty to the brand and company as employees will find unity together. It can also increase productivity, reduce absences, and result in longer retention as employees will feel closer together.

On the down side, if people do not get along or when someone is not pulling their weight it can create quite a bit of anxiety and resentment within a team. Hence the importance of managing situations in a time efficient manner.

HR JAIL: I was once placed on a project team to create a training model that was going to be launched for the whole organization. The company had wanted this training module for some time, yet it seemed the senior executives had been procrastinating. Then when it came time to for our executives to pitch the idea to the board of directors everything moved in sixth gear. The project team was created, with specific goals and a very aggressive three-month timeline for completion. Most of my colleagues and I did not live and work in the same area, therefore we committed to weekly Skype sessions to divide up our tasks, report back on our progress, and/or seek out help if needed. There were four of us on this project, and we did not have extra hands to share the workload.

Our first month into the project was geared towards market research, ensuring we were going to have a competitive training module that would be value added and relevant. On our first few Skype sessions everything seemed to go smoothly, everyone was engaged, helping each other, recognizing each other. By the end of our first month, we started to see a gap in information. Three out of the four members would be sharing the work they did via email, asking for guidance from each other, yet there was an odd feeling from one member even though he verbally always told us he was on target. As we are all adults, you would assume babysitting was not necessary and if someone was struggling they would ask for help.

Six weeks in, when we needed to provide a rough draft of our material then the truth came out. We had an internal hard drive where we could upload our documents, and we had committed as a team to only upload items once we felt they were ready to view by our leader since it was on the drive our leader could access the information. We had our six-week checkpoint Skype call and three out of four employees had produced their work. The fourth employee had every excuse under the sun and our leader was believing him. It was demotivating and ridiculously frustrating at the same time.

After our update call with our leader, the three of us got on our own call and devised a plan. If this guy was screwing around for six weeks, we had six weeks of stuff to catch up on, and there was no way we were going to get penalized for his laziness and/or inabilities. Our first step was to give our colleague one get out of jail free card, aka a chance. We had a four-way Skype call, laid everything on the line, and it was apparent this colleague was lying through his teeth. He had done nothing, and we did not believe he felt bad nor would he catch up. Instead of bringing this to our leader now, we decided to re-divide the work between three of us and increase our speed. The fourth colleague was still invited to Skype calls, still recommended to share work although we paid little attention to him. For all intents and purposes he did not exist. We believed it was easier to deal with the issue rather than look like fools in front of our board of directors. Three months in, we placed our work on the drive, had a call with our leader and waited for the board to review our work. During our call with our leader, this fourth member was very quiet, even when our leader praised us for our great work the fourth member was included in their praise yet he never said a word, nor did we. A few weeks later, the board's decision came in. They loved the training module, wanted a few minor tweaks then it would be ready to launch within the whole organization. After we completed our final version we decided to write a letter to our leader to explain the situation and request that the bonus structure be divided in three and not in four as the fourth member did not contribute. We included emails we had exchanged, which were date and time stamped, plus other evidence demonstrating the fourth member's lack of collaboration.

In the end, we not only got our bonus divided by three, we also got a mini getaway for three nights and four days as our leader explained to the board what had happened and they were impressed with our work and professionalism throughout the project. This mini getaway did not cost the company much money as they owned the resorts where our getaway was taking place. Yet that is not the point of sharing my story. We were happy with just having the bonus divided in three; the added resort getaway was icing on top of our cake. Can you imagine how engaged the three of us were? That is a story I have proudly told many for years.

I was later fortunate for the turnout of this situation and not every situation has such a positive ending. That later six weeks was a struggle, lack of sleep, I had a caught a cold for almost four weeks, and I was not eating properly since I was so focused on getting this done. I am not recommending someone to have their health suffer for a work project yet I am trying to demonstrate that there are times where people are not going to pull their weight in group work, even group incentivized work and should something like my situation happen to you, you will need to decide your best course of action not only for the short term but more importantly, the long term.

C: Company Bonus Structure

This is a very common method of bonus for organizations. They are frequently combined with part individual and part company bonus models. This allows employees to gain a little something extra if the company is doing well, without placing a company in bankruptcy mode should it not be doing well. After all, it is better to have a job with no bonus than no job at all. The way a company bonus structure is calculated also varies based on the level of your position. It could be a percentage of your salary just like the individual bonus; it could be profit sharing, stock options, and even a combination of all of them. With profit sharing, for example, a company would set aside 2.5 up to 15 per cent of their labour budget to use for a bonus should the company be profitable. Profit sharing also helps with having employees understand how the business works, as they get to see their own performance reflect on the company's performance. Employees tend to feel more responsibility and loyalty to a company when they are part of the company. Again, they have skin in the game.

No matter the method you choose for your business, you can also place a cap on the bonus and set limits on the company bonus structure. Setting limits can also help with forecasting your budgets and ensuring the bonus is reasonable for you and the company.

There are a few other bonus structures that exist within businesses. A sign-on bonus when you are hired means you are given a certain amount of money in exchange for a set amount of years of service and the employee is meant to remain in good standing to obtain the bonus. Milestone bonuses are when an employee goes above and beyond, completes a project that perhaps may not have been part of their regular duties and they are given a onetime cash bonus. Retention bonuses tend to occur in a merger or acquisition as you want an employee to stay on for a period of time. I would not recommend these in a regular workplace. If an employee wants to jump ship, and they are looking elsewhere, a onetime bonus is a Band-Aid and will not keep them engaged for long – it is usually a waste of money in the long run.

Vacation and Sick Pay

Vacation Pay

Legislation frequently pre-determines what you are required to pay for a vacation percentage. Whether it is four per cent, which is two weeks a year, six per cent, which is three weeks a year or if you are part of the European Union most countries have eight per cent, which is four weeks year for a total of 20 working days. If you are lucky you are in New Zealand or France with a required 30 days per year, or Austria with 35 days per year. In some parts of the world there is no required vacation time. There is a consistent debate about the productivity level for employees who take vacation time versus the ones who do not. Many countries have done studies to support their method of legislation. What is important to you as a leader and/or business owner is that you follow your law. Should your law not require you to provide paid vacation, it would certainly be in your best interest to keep your employees engaged and be a desired employer.

Every business should have a method to request time off and track time off that is well communicated and documented. This process should be part of your employee handbook and regular policies that employees sign off on upon hire and perhaps even on a yearly basis. If you are a small- to medium-sized employer you will most likely use an Excel spreadsheet. If you can afford to, I would suggest something electronic as it is easier for leaders to manage in the long run.

**Remember! Your vacation budget
is part of your labour budget.**

When you are reviewing your annual budget, keep in mind that your vacation budget is part of your labour budget. If you are providing your employees with two weeks paid vacation, this means that employees are paid 52 weeks in a year, and only physically working 50 weeks a year. This also means that 50 paid weeks are part of your regular labour budget while two paid weeks are part of your vacation budget. In the end, it is all the same budget, yet your vacation budget is like a bank, it tends to keep accumulating if not used on a yearly basis. Therefore, you should also include a stipulation in your policy that vacation must be taken on a yearly basis. If you do not want an employee to collect six weeks of vacation monies in their bank because it will be hard for most employers to replace someone for a six-week period throughout a year this needs to be documented. Also, I would not recommend paying out an employee's vacation while also allowing them to work. This could almost be double pay. If an employee is meant to leave the business for two weeks per year and they will get paid out of their vacation monies, what happens when they also work those two weeks, which means the employee worked a total of 52 weeks in a calendar year plus you paid them out the two weeks' vacation monies that was in their vacation bank. This could cost you more money.

Logically think about it: you have now paid someone 54 weeks that calendar year when they worked 52 weeks. Be careful not to make this mistake. Some of you may be thinking that if an employee does not want to take vacation and work through their vacation you can pay them their vacation monies as they are working through their vacation. Make life simple for you. If you are working, you are paid from your regular budget, when you are on vacation not in your business you are paid from your vacation budget and do not mix the two. Do not pay out someone's vacation time; ensure they physically take time off from the business to relax and rejuvenate.

Sick Pay

This too may be governed by your legislation. Laws are slowly changing around the world and businesses are forced to have paid sick leave for employees of all status. The amount of sick days required varies, and you have to keep in the mind the increased cost this is to your business. You have employees who will take all their allotted sick days and then you may need to call in for backup. Depending on your type of business, calling for backup may be easy or non-existent. If non-existent are you prepared to run shorthanded? You will be paying someone while they are off plus paying someone to replace them while they are off.

There are general administration costs to administer sick time as it takes up a leader's time to document the time off, find the replacement, and even manage the employee should there be a concern with attendance and punctuality. You also have to include a policy as to what sick time can be used for. Will you allow your employees to use it freely for their own personal illness, they have a dentist appointment, etc.? Or will it be just for the employee themselves. What if their child is sick? This is something else to add to your employee policies.

As far as appreciation goes, having paid sick time is a positive message to employees and also relieves some of the burden if someone truly is sick knowing they can recover at home and not get anyone else sick at work. There are also some countries that decide to pay sick time based on their social security contributions, and employees contribute to their sick fund by automatic deductions from their pay.

How will you – if at all – recognize your employees who never take their sick time? Will there be an incentive for employees and if so is this appropriate for your type of business or can this send the wrong message to your employees? Will people who take sick time be penalized by not being able to take part in the extra incentives? Will your sick time have any monetary value, such that if employees do not take it, it gets paid out? I would not suggest this, as again it may send the wrong message. You will see an increase in abuse; employees will lie as they would prefer payment and it would cost your business more money.

On average, only about 60 per cent of staff use their sick time on a yearly basis, therefore you have 40 per cent of your budget that you could save. Lastly, will there be an opportunity to carry over time from year to year. If you provide your employees with four sick days per year, if they do not use them one year, can they be banked for the following year? If you allow carryover, will you have a limit to this carryover? If you are not sure, I would suggest having a limit. It is a nice benefit to have yet it also needs to have structure and parameters for the best use of the benefit.

Other Benefits

There are many other benefits you should consider offering your employees in addition to those you may be required to offer.

Consideration

Health and Dental: These tend to cost a company quite a bit of money. However, it is very common for an employer to offer these benefits, especially when you want to be competitive in the market. They are usually offered to full-time and salaried employees, yet I have known some companies to extend them to part-time and even contract employees. There are many plans with different providers you would need to look into. Usually, you would not offer the same package to all levels of employees. As an example, a more senior person could get a better benefit plan at a lower cost as the employer would "recognize" the senior employee and cover a larger portion of the benefit plan premiums. Prior to committing to anything, do your homework. Perhaps even seek out the assistance of a benefit consultant. If you choose to offer health and dental, I would suggest to break down the premium fees so that you can use the cost analysis during your recruitment and/ or performance appraisal process.

For example: If the cost of benefits for an employee of a particular position is $45 per month and the employer pays $25 of that $45, that leaves the employee paying $20 per month for their plan. With some governments, the fees an employee pays for benefits is a taxable benefit, which is therefore also something to look into. If that employee made $18 per hour, the result is the employee is actually making $18.16 per hour due to the employer's portion of the premium costs ($25/150 hours working per month = 0.16 cents more per hour. The 150 hours is 37.5 hours per week x 4 weeks = 150 hours per month). The cost of providing health and dental is certainly something you would want to include as part of your Total Rewards package as it is a selling point for recruitment and retention.

Maternity/Paternity, Adoption Leave Top Up: This type of benefit is also becoming more popular to offer in the workplace. You first need to create an eligibility process for the top-up, e.g. the employee is to be in good standing for a minimum of two consecutive years and they need to have two years of consecutive tenure. Then you decide if you will top-up to 75 per cent or maybe even 100 per cent of one salary and determine the length of this top up: 6 months, 1 year. If the employee is hourly then you take an average of their salary based on 8–12 weeks.

———

Remember! Maternity/Paternity leave is a contract; be sure to specify all benefits and consequences so that it is very clear for both the employee and employer what all conditions are.

———

Also, review your legislation as you may have a specific calculation you need to follow. In most legislation, a top-up is not required by law therefore you have full control over what you want to offer and for how long. What legislation frequently dictates is that the employee must be given the mat leave benefit for the period of time legislation determines and the leave must be job protected (meaning the employee cannot be replaced and must be able to come back to the same job or that of similar duties when they return). You also should have a few precautionary clauses in your policy, e.g. the employee must return to work for a minimum of six months or one year once the leave is completed. Should they choose to resign they will need to payback the top-up. Should they request to step down or extend their leave, no guarantees can be made and decisions will be based on the needs of the business. This Maternity/Paternity leave is a contract; be sure to specify all benefits and consequences so that it is very clear for both the employee and employer what all conditions are.

Potential Legislative Requirements

Life, Disability, Accidental Death and Dismemberment Insurance: The are insurance policies that usually pay benefits to a beneficiary should a life-threatening incident occur and the employee can no longer return to work. It is usually not an expensive policy to have in your business; in some companies the employer pays all the premiums, and in others it is a shared cost. Just like health and dental, with some governments, this may be a taxable benefit, hence something to keep in mind.

There are many stipulations that define the eligibility and payout process under the Accidental Death and Dismemberment policy. The incident must be accidental, the portion paid out is a percentage of one's annual salary usually in the form of one lump sum.

Family and Medical Leave, Military Leave, Jury Duty, Religious Observance, Bereavement, Short-Term Disability, Long-Term Disability and other leave which may be required by legislation: Review what you are required to do, add your requirements to your employee handbook and as you grow and develop consider including other types of leave that may not be required by law yet are a benefit to your employees and can assist with engagement.

Everything Else

The intrinsic benefits, or as I call them the "everything else", is what I believe to be the most important part of your business. People accept a job because of what they see on the outside, the extrinsic benefits, yet people stay in a job and/or with an organization because of how they feel on the inside; the intrinsic benefits. For as many years as can be documented employees want to be challenged, they want to learn, grow and develop, they want to be perceived to be meaningful and want to feel that they are part of a company. Many of these emotions do come from within such as self-motivation, personal ambition, and drive. Yet it is the role of a leader and an organization to add fuel to this ambition, to help keep this drive going. You need to get to know your employees, know what makes them happy and do what you can to keep them happy. When someone is happy in the workplace, they feel a sense of achievement, they feel successful and success is one of those intrinsic rewards. What would you prefer: your employees to come in to work, do their job for eight hours then leave or come in to work, laugh and chat with others, support and help others, provide suggestions for improvement or new ways of thinking, go home, tell their family about another awesome day at work, like and even share something about your company on social media. I think it is an easy choice to make. Then it is yours to create. The culture and environment at your business is directly related to the intrinsic benefits that keep employees motivated.

A few examples you can implement in your workplace are:

- ✓ Regular check-in with employees to keep them challenged and engaged. Perhaps once a quarter you have a 15-minute face to face. Focus on two things: What's working and what's not. You give the opportunity for the employee to tell you what they like, so that you can give them more (if it's within reason and the needs of the business) and what's not working so perhaps you can take this off their plate.

- ✓ Words of praise from Leaders. It does not have to be often yet most people feel absolutely wonderful when their boss or even their boss's boss gives them a shout out for something they have done. That amazing successful feeling will resonate with that employee for months. Praise has to be divided between people, departments, and not always the same person.

- ✓ Freedom and Autonomy – if you are nagging at your employees all the time you create anxiety and pressure. Give your employees a task, give them a deadline, point them in the right direction and always advise them they are to come to you if they have questions. Then let them go! People are more resourceful than you think. If you stay on top of things too much you are micromanaging, resulting in making people dependent on you. This will not work for you in the long run. You might as well do the work yourself as this is how it will turn out.

- ✓ If you offer employees their birthday day off with pay, summer half-day Friday's so work stops at 1:00 p.m. – these are perks that become part of your Total Rewards package.

We will go into much more detail about recognition in the Employee Engagement section, and you will then see how all facets of HR are connected.

Total Rewards Takeaways

- ✓ Total Rewards is the package of offerings you provide to an employee in exchange for their hard work in your place of business. They are categorized by #1 Money and #2 Everything Else

- ✓ Labour is your most expensive expenditure, at least 40–70 per cent of your overall budget

- ✓ Staying competitive in the market is key to attracting and retaining talent

- ✓ Determine your core Total Rewards package at the onset and expand/develop the package as your business expands

- ✓ Offer fair and reasonable monetary compensation and don't cheap out on the "Everything Else"

- ✓ Always review your legislation to ensure you are offering what you are required to do and choose to be an employer of choice and offer a little more

- ✓ Giving employees the opportunity to have "skin in the game" such as eligibility to an individual and company bonus provides not only financial recognition yet, more importantly, it shows appreciation

CHAPTER 4

TRAINING AND DEVELOPMENT

The more training and knowledge an employee has, the better opportunity for promotions, resulting in greater self-satisfaction

---

Training and development is the investment you make in your people. It may sound humble of you to want to invest in your people yet there are good reasons for you to do so. It will directly benefit your business as employees can do more work with less margin for error. It will fill their need for the intrinsic benefits – the "Everything Else" as well as the extrinsic benefits "Money". Employees will feel more competent and useful, thus more engaged. Employees will require less supervision, and it will also reduce turnover. The more training and knowledge an employee has the better opportunity for promotions, resulting in greater self-satisfaction and possibility of more money. On average, companies spend 15–35 hours per employee per year on training. This could be due to a new company process being put in place, legislated training that was required or perhaps job shadowing for another role. In some countries, companies are required to have a training "bank" for an employee where the employee accumulates time that the company must allow the employee to devote to training. With these types of situations, that company is required to donate a percentage of their payroll to this training bank. This can cost businesses anywhere from $1,000 to upwards of $3–4,000 per person per year. For example, if you were introducing a new process into your business, factor in the time it takes for the leader to learn the new process, then to train their direct reports, add the leader's wages plus the employee's wages for this time frame, and it does not stop there. You also usually have an amount of back and forth between leader to employee for continuous coaching. In the end, everyone's time costs money.

There are different components to training and development in the workplace: onboarding and required training, self-development and career development. The ultimate goals for training to help your employees gain new skills and abilities are to improve their performance and to achieve their career goals. So how do you decide what training programs and/or materials you need for your business?

- ✓ Training programs you use must match your company's culture. If the work environment such as people's behaviours and performance do not support the training initiative, then there is no point in implementing the training.
- ✓ If the senior leadership in your organization do not walk the talk, then why waste your time?

✓ Any training program your company introduces must be relevant, if your company's culture and expectations change, the training must adapt as well.

✓ Keep in mind people learn differently. Some prefer lecture style, role play, simulations, one-on-one conversation and many people like audio-visual. Generally, people have an idea of what they prefer yet for your benefit include a little variety in each training system and regularly communicate with your employees to ensure they are grasping the training.

✓ If change management is your current focus, look to the role-playing method as it's known to be the most effective since it gives the opportunity for employees to connect with their feelings, which helps change attitudes and develop interpersonal skills.

✓ Consider how much money are you required and/or can afford to invest. If you do not have a government requirement then you can look into having a small education fund for your employees to use to help subsidize a cost of a course. This could be anywhere from a few hundred dollars per year to several thousand. If you choose this method you want to include strict guidelines on what the money can be used for. Do the funds accumulate year over year, or must they be used on a yearly basis?

✓ You can choose to do group training, where you decide the topic/module you want your employees to take, you organize the day, pay for the trainer and schedule your employees to take the course. This may be a more cost-effective way for a business, especially when you are starting out.

✓ There are also many companies that offer development courses on-line, which is something you can offer to your employees. You usually pay an initial fee upfront around a few thousand dollars, then a per user fee anywhere from $20–$75 per month. If you choose off the shelf training, I would suggest you to start with a trial period prior to making a full-time commitment. A great way to engage your employees is to include the training in your company requirements for your employees so that they take a certain number of courses per year to ensure you are getting a return on your investment. You can also ask all employees to do the same course, give them a deadline of say 60 days, then at the end of the 60 days have a brainstorming/ meeting to review the learnings of the course and how they should be applied to your company.

When you think of your employee's training life cycle, onboarding and required training is your first step. It includes a combination of company and legislative required training. Let's examine these together.

Onboarding and Required Training

✓ You created a 2–3 day orientation that any new employee in your organization needs to go through. You reviewed things such as new hire paperwork, vacation process, company values and mission, customer service philosophy, etc. This training will allow you to cover general company policies, procedures, privacy and confidentiality, safety and security policies.

✓ You also included required legislative training: Workplace Violence and Harassment, Occupational Health and Safety, and if applicable Accessibility for Persons with Disabilities.

✓ Then you have a 2-day specific departmental checklist of items to review.

✓ By Day 6 is when you tailor the training slightly to more focused OJT (on-the-job training). Depending on how much previous knowledge and experience your new employee has it could be a matter of starting from scratch, or having to "brandify" your employee to your business.

✓ After an average of two to three weeks, the new employee will solely need some coaching and regular check-ins.

———

To foster a positive working relationship, the majority of the time you should take the collaborative approach.

———

What are coaching and regular check-ins? Over the years, I have noticed how shy people are, maybe even nervous to ask questions or make it known that they are confused or lost. This is where the leader is tasked with responsibilities to take the first step, and even the second and third step in helping your employees. Leaders must approach employees, ask questions and offer assistance, i.e. check in. There is often an atmosphere where "if you are an adult then you should act like one and come to me if you need something." This is not a fair expectation of a new employee and sometimes not fair for any employee. It depends on your organization what generation of people you employ. Therefore, conduct your check-ins. A check-in is not a hello how are you. You are looking to see if someone is understanding training, therefore you need to be specific. How did you find the training? Is there anything you are unsure about? What would you change about the training if anything? Never assume that someone understands something the first time around. A leader is a coach by default and should you have direct reports or not, there is a time to be a boss (more directive) and a time to be a coach (more collaborative). For the purposes of training and development, a leader should not be directive, nor should you take the boss approach because you need to allow the individual to learn. When a leader is directive there is no learning, it is simply an individual doing what they are told. There are a few times in a business when a leader is to be directive, however to foster a positive working relationship, the majority of the time you should take the collaborative approach.

You also have to keep in mind we all learn at different paces and through different methods. It is leaders and organizations who must adapt to the market and climate, not solely an employee. As a leader, it is your job to adapt your style to suit the individual you are with. When you are with a group, then you would follow a 'majority' rule.

———

Remember! Check your ego at the door!

———

Story Time:

> I've worked in Human Resources for over 15 years and in people management for approximately 20, and the one thing that is recurring for leaders new and old, that continues to trip them up time after time is something that only they have control over ... their ego. Coaching new leaders, my first piece of advice is consistently – check your ego at the door. As a new leader you are excited, nervous, and perhaps even anxious, about the new leadership role ahead. You have a team reporting to you, looking at you for leadership,

direction, inspiration, and guidance. It can be quite over-
whelming with such a big step up in expectations. It's not
just about you anymore – looking after yourself, controlling
your emotions, setting expectations for yourself – you have a
team with all eyes on you. The responsibility, accountability,
and the power that comes with a people leadership role can
be overwhelming, but it can also be intoxicating. Don't get
me wrong, we all have an ego and like to feel strong, confi-
dent and powerful, but if you let this power go to your head,
you will soon have a team that will be displaying mutiny
and having you walk the plank.

I can recall a leader I worked with in recent years; let's call
him Bob. Bob was in charge of a large Business Unit, with
500+ team members. Bob was reporting to the CEO of the
company. Bob was a very intelligent man, with a technical
degree and decades of experience. But what struck me the
first time I met him (as his HR Business Partner or HRBP)
and every interaction we had for the next two years, was
how big his ego was. He had many General Managers
reporting to him, but his ego got in his way with regard
to his leadership style. He was a cocky senior executive but
couldn't lead effectively. He was afraid of confrontation,
and wouldn't have the tough, courageous conversations that
he needed to. It was the constructive performance feedback
conversations with his General Managers that he avoided.
So what happened? The problem festered, and got worse
and worse, to the point where the General Managers were
not effective leaders, and their team culture deteriorated to
the point where team members were crying at their desks.
I had provided Bob advice many times that he needed

to intervene early, and provide constructive feedback to help his General Managers improve their performance and ultimately their leadership skills. Unfortunately, Bob washed over my advice and ultimately we had to bring in an external Industrial Relations company and a number of psychologists to intervene. Early intervention is key, and would've avoided this becoming a much larger industrial mess than it needed to be. I am no longer Bob's HRBP, I have moved on to another Business Unit with a much more humble senior executive. I wish I could say that Bob has changed, but after so many decades of letting his ego control him, versus the other way around, unfortunately he hasn't.

Demonstrate 'confident humility' as your leadership style.

I have read many articles about leadership over the years, and the one constant piece of advice is to demonstrate humility. Being humble, modest, again checking the ego at the door is a valuable quality to live by. Look back at your past; there will be (hopefully) one great leader that you have worked with. Someone you have learned from who was truly effective and added value, but more importantly, they were a great person that lived by their values, and most probably ... were humble. We all remember the leaders with the big egos that we worked with, and to be honest, you probably don't rate them very highly. If you truly want to stand out and be the leader that you would want to follow, demonstrate 'confident humility' as your leadership style. You need to display a level of confidence, not cockiness; you are a leader after all. But don't be over the top and let the power go to your head; show some humility and set the example. Remember, all eyes are on you.

My advice – get a mentor, someone who is more experienced than you, who has been down this path and made mistakes, owned them, learned from them and become even more experienced because of this; someone you can see is both confident and humble. Ask them questions, show some vulnerability, be human, and be open to advice.

Damian

15+ years of experience in Human Resources

Australia

When a person is interested in learning new things, they will be driven by their own self-interest. This tends to be one of the easiest ways to learn, as a person needs to want to learn if they will actually retain and apply what they have learned. As a leader, you do not necessarily need to be involved with someone's own self-development, yet you would be there as a support, encouragement, and sometimes guidance.

Self-Development

- ✓ You can have a library of books available to be signed out for a period of time.
- ✓ Create the education fund we talked about above for employees to use with certain stipulations.
- ✓ Post bulletins about your community centers, surrounding colleges and even from your own organization that offer outside courses sometimes free or at a minimal cost.

✓ Talk to your employees about their interests as you could tie in their personal interests for self-development into their career development. Keep in mind, not every employee wants a career at your place of business, however you will not know until you ask.

✓ Support your employees; allow them to adapt their schedule for personal development, have them talk about their initiatives at team meetings.

There are countless stories of how people learn things on their own because they have drive – when someone knew nothing about a particular topic and they made it their mission to read every book and apply what they have learned that now they can be considered subject matter experts. Self-development is a very powerful feeling. It's the "superman and superwomen" feeling: "I can do anything, I can conquer the world."

I like the "Nasty Gal" story, it is a fairly modern story therefore relatable to our current environment. Sophia Amoruso started her company from scratch buying vintage clothing at second hand, used stores and selling them on an online EBay store. Her company did so well that she ended up on the Forbes self-made millionaire list. However, in a few short years, the company became a bad HR story. Several employees came forth, filed lawsuits and made complaints of mistreatment. There were articles claiming the environment was toxic, which were due to an absent Sophia and CEO named Sheree Waterson. It seems Sophia was more concerned with being famous than running her company. She eventually had to file for bankruptcy. There are so many speculations one could make as to why such a successful company died so quickly. The main lessen to learn is that employees are any business's most valuable asset. Treat them even better than the way you treat your customers.

Career Development

Every organization should have some form of career development available to its employees. Part of this career development is a structured process where at minimum one time per year you discuss an employee's career goals and how they can complement those of your business. This discussion would usually take place at the same time as a performance appraisal. You could document parts of this conversation on your performance appraisal form, however it is recommended to have a separate career development document. Why? If you are setting small targets to help someone build their tool belt to get to the next role, you will be reviewing that employee's progress or lack thereof several times a quarter or at least per year. Using a separate tool for this, one that you can add to a performance appraisal would be easier for you to manage. What does such a career development plan tool look like?

Step 1: Introduction Letter

Welcome to the (insert company name) career development toolkit. You have now gained one to two years of experience with our company, and you are looking towards your next move. This toolkit is to be used as a starting point to assess your current competencies and generate avenues to explore your options for your future.

Your role as the leader is to determine the motive/interest for wanting a career change and if the person has self-awareness into their own skills and abilities. This can help you decide if the employee is ready, which is a necessary first step in career management as you are both investing time and money into this process. You want what is best for your employee and business.

Step 2: Reflection

1. Why did you choose (insert job title)?

2. What career ideas and plans did you have at the start of (insert job title)?

3. Did anybody influence you to obtain this (insert job title / choose this career path)?

4. What do you believe are your current strengths and opportunities in (insert job title)?

5. Based on your answers what are your reasons for wanting a career move?

You need to have an open and honest conversation with realistic questions about the employee's desire for a role compared to the actual possibilities of that employee getting to where they want.

Step 3: Career Analysis Review

1. What are your achievements since you have been in (insert job title)?

2. What specific experience have you gained that has assisted with your development?

3. What do you enjoy most and least about the role?

4. Who have you enjoyed working with and why?

5. If you could choose 3–4 tasks you would like to continue doing as you enjoy them and you believe they are your strengths, what would they be?

The reflection and job analysis is completed. As a leader, this is where you do most of your work helping to plan the career development of each employee. Can you add this employee to a succession planning tree? If so, would they be ready in one year, two years or three years? What skills, courses, and job shadowing do they need to be ready in the allotted time frame? You can have a simple template such as the one below to track the items you believe this employee needs to learn and courses they should take to prepare themselves. It's important to have a specific timeline as to when the task/course needs to be completed by and, most importantly, a coach.

Coaches: A coach is someone who usually already has perfected the task, skill or course the employee is going to do. It is not necessarily the highest tenured employee. Remember, we reviewed in the onboarding that if you have a fellow colleague teach others anything, they need to be taught first. This is called train the trainer. This same methodology should take place for a coach. A coach needs to first and foremost agree to be a coach. Not every person has this interest, nor is just anyone good at being a coach. Prior to assigning a career development coach, engage in that conversation, train the coach on what you want them to help others with, then support from afar.

Step 4: Plan Development

Insert Name: _____ Hire Date: _____			
Position: _____			
Course / Skill / Task to develop	**Coach's Name**	**Timeline / Date to review**	**Notes, Date of Notes**
Management Leadership course	Jane Doe	60 days – It's good to include a specific date	Use this section to track the progress or lack thereof
One Minute Manager meets the Monkey	Bob Smith	90 days	"
Job Shadowing 2 hours per day	Lori Cole	3 months	"

Once you have followed the above three steps, you can certainly add other steps to this process based on your organization's needs. The key will be to conduct your follow-up. The Timeline / Date to Review you include in your plan development supports your integrity as a leader and directly affects the success of your employee. If you say you will meet your employee on a specific date, please do so. Do not take vacation, schedule a meeting or find something else to do on that day. It is very disappointing to an employee when their leader talks and does not follow through with actions, especially when it comes to someone's career.

Story Time:

I worked with someone who had big aspirations for his career with the company we both worked for. His name is Jack. He would stay late after work, come in early, always put his hand up to help someone, take on a new project, and genuinely wanted to learn. He was well liked by all fellow colleagues, customers wanted to deal with him specifically and was overall a fun guy to be around. After about a year and a half, Jack finally had the career conversation with his manager, who acknowledged his work ethic and verbally told him he would see what he could do to help him get more exposure to senior roles to assess his abilities and interests. After about a month or so, Jack got his "new development assignment". He was given the duty to coach three other fellow leaders who had been struggling who had similar roles and responsibilities to him. His assignment was for three months and at the end of the three months his leader was going to obtain feedback from Jack's colleagues as well as from Jack himself. At no time was Jack advised by his leader there would be progress meetings in between the three months.

As I sat back and watched how excited Jack was for his additional new duties, he was like a kid in a candy store. He was so happy, full of energy and felt like superman. His coaching seemed to start off well, we would talk about how his day went, he would ask me for HR advice and all seemed to be on track. Several weeks in, I bumped into a colleague who was getting Jack's coaching – we will call him Steve. Steve asked me out for coffee, and he wanted it to be off company premises. In HR, when someone wants to meet you outside of work, it is not to talk about life, it is to bitch about work, ask for advice and/or report something that has happened. Needless to say, I was slightly anxious and curious at the same time. Anxious, because Jack and I were work friends, we got along well and I was so happy for him to have this opportunity, and although I have had many difficult conversations with my friends, there was something that just didn't feel right.

Steve and I met for coffee, and Steve spilled the beans. He felt Jack was a selfish know-it-all, cocky son of a bitch who walked in his department telling him and two other colleagues what to do. Steve was so upset that once he started talking he barely came up for air for over 20 minutes. I sat there in shock sipping my latte quietly, my eyebrows raised and all I did was nod my head. When Steve was finally done his rant I asked him why he wanted to meet me for coffee – was it because he wanted to blow off steam or because I am friends with Jack or because I am in HR, and he wanted to make a complaint. This is part of the responsibility HR professionals have. You never know if people are coming to you as fellow colleagues or because of your title. It's important to make that clear distinction so that these coffee meets, or water cooler conversations do not get used against you. Just your presence in a meeting, or even at the same coffee shop can be turned around; this can happen to any leader not just an HR leader. Any leader for that matter should always ask what someone's intentions are when they spill the beans.

In Steve's case, he had not thought that far and as we talked he finally decided that he wanted me as Jack's friend to see if I could help without having to get senior leadership involved. Since the issue was not against safety, security, or breaking any laws, I was able to follow through with Steve's request. I spoke with Jack and let him know that "I heard" his approach may not be well received and perhaps he could be more engaging, and collaborative in his coaching and less of a top down approach. What I did not see was that these extra duties that Jack was tasked with went to his head. Somehow, between the conversation he had been having with his leader, Jack believed all he needed to do was these extra duties for three months, and he was getting a promotion. Being in HR, I knew it was not that easy to get a promotion yet it became very clear to me that Jack did not listen nor was he advised of the process. There was a process in place that Jack was not yet taking part in. Jack ended up resenting me, thinking I was jealous that he was going to get a promotion and I was still in the same position for a few years. He did not want to listen to my advice or my knowledge of the company procedures for career development. We lost our friendship because of this, yet the way I see it, if Jack and I were true friends we would still be friends. The lessons I learned from this situation:

- ✓ Jack's leader built Jack up about the potential of his career development, without consulting HR and without any formal career development documentation, thus leading to what I believe became Jack's hothead attitude.

- ✓ I should not have approached Jack. I should have gone to Jack's leader right away to help his leader, advise him he needed to follow the career development process, and ensure there were progress reports scheduled every few weeks with both Jack and the three colleagues he was coaching.

- ✓ Jack should have realized that being a leader, mentor and coach means that nothing is about you anymore. He was so consumed with getting a promotion that he forgot to be the nice awesome guy he was known for being. He made it all about him and in the end it led him to failure.

This was a valuable lesson for me to be part of and observe. When you are a leader, you are there to help others, guide others, and support others. That is the role of a leader. As soon as you become selfish, self-centered and forget your purpose as a leader you lose. Once you lose, you might as well leave, perhaps even quit and start over. Someone's reputation is their brand, their legacy and once you break it, it is *sooooo* hard to get back.

Step 5: Opportunities

Now is the time to decide which opportunity you can give someone should their development plan have gone well. Telling the truth is important. Do not string someone along if they are not capable, or not yet ready for the next move. You should only get to this step once you have openly communicated with the employee. You need to be a role model, encourage conversations about career development and coaching and ensure leaders have the knowledge and authority to offer career development opportunities to people within their team.

The four main types of opportunities are:

A: Growing in place: This is when you give someone new tasks, added duties to their role that will keep them engaged and also develop their skills and abilities. This is not usually temporary, however a slight change in one's job description usually also results in additional compensation.

B: Lateral moves: This is for someone who is not quite ready for the move up, or if there are no current promotion opportunities and/ or when you would prefer the employee obtain more company exposure, work with different people, or perhaps even a different department. A title may change, yet the money and status usually stays the same.

C: Moving up: This is a promotion, usually within one's field, allowing someone to work in an area they know well, which provides an increase in responsibility, status, and pay. Cross pollination exists here, including moving to different departments.

D: Realignment: This could be an opportunity to move away from tasks or responsibilities the employee no longer wants; sometimes the employee's title will change as will part of their job description and/or they may even change location.

Next Steps:

» Once you have gotten to the opportunity step, there should be a formal method of documenting that the employee is officially taking part in career development and what the timeline is, if any.

» If the person is taking a new role B, C or D a new offer letter must be signed.

» If the role is more senior there could be additional documents to be signed such as a non-compete clause, different benefit opportunities, e.g. pension.

» A formal announcement to the team and business should be released in a timely fashion.

» Maybe even have a small cake and card. It is important to recognize career development within your business. When someone wants to stay with you, and be loyal to you, you should thank them for that.

Generational Differences

There are many other things that are relevant to leaders in a business. One of my suggested most important aspects is connected to generational differences. Understanding your client, who in fact is your employee, is crucial to the success of your department and organization. Employing and training people from all backgrounds and generations is great for diverse experience and knowledge yet can also cause departmental anxiety and interpersonal problems. When we do not understand each other, we react in a negative way. When someone is not communicating with you the way you like, you get your back up, think it's disrespectful when in fact there may be nothing wrong with the style of communication, it is just different from yours.

Take for example a Baby Boomer Brenda and a Gen Z Julia who are working on a project together. The Baby Boomer Brenda wants to meet at work to discuss the project, divide up the work, come up with a strategic plan and is okay to even stay late if the meeting does not accomplish everything needed. The Gen Z Julia wants to meet at a coffee shop, also during work hours, informally decide who is doing what verbally, no need to document or write anything up, then for the remainder of the meeting chit chat about life. Brenda feels that Julia doesn't care, is not serious about the project and Julia feels like she wants to enjoy herself while working. Julia does not understand why working in a coffee shop is not as valuable as working in their office. Then Brenda is going to talk to her colleague friends and say things like "kids these days have no work ethic". Julia will talk to her colleague friends and say "Brenda is living in the dinosaur age; she has no clue how to enjoy life". Then gossip happens, the project will most likely not continue and they may even end up complaining to their leader or even HR. Examples like this happen multiple times a day around the world. In this example, both employees get upset, feel offended and over what

… miscommunication and not understanding one another. The style of communication, how an individual is motivated, leadership preferences, the definition of collaboration, adapting to change and gaining technical skills all vary from one generation to the next. This is why training all employees on accepting and embracing generational differences is important to your business.

JLP Tip: When I have assigned people to projects or working teams, I purposely assign people from different generations. Prior to commencing I would go over some tips on each generation/person's preferences, dislikes. I also remind people to not take things personally. We are all doing what we think is right or is best. If our actions or words are wrong, then this is where coaching and mentoring should take place.

Let's take a look at the differences between generations to better assist you as a leader.

Skills	Baby Boomer 1946–1964	Gen X 1965-1976	Gen Y Millenials 1977–1995	Gen Z 1996–Now
Communication	Diplomatic, formal, reserved, wait to offer opinion until asked, preference is face to face or over telephone only, like to establish a friendly rapport, believe in allowing high tenured people to communicate first, i.e. they know best	Will share thoughts face to face, blunt and direct, present facts, emphasize the WIFM, trying to have work life balance and not be on their phone 24/7, ask them for their input, do not tell. Look for competence, and will listen to those who are perceived as competent, likes public recognition		Relaxed, casual, do not call, they will not answer. Text and will respond within minutes. If face to face, skeptical but like it when it happens just not used to it. High speed stimulus junkies, want to be recognized by knowing they matter, need more guidance and feedback

Skills	Baby Boomer 1946–1964	Gen X 1965-1976	Gen Y Millenials 1977–1995	Gen Z 1996–Now
Adapting	Take time to adapt, may be cynical to change, need to understand the why, very loyal once there is buy-in	Embrace Change. May be skeptical but will adapt once they understand the why. If they do not understand they will not support it. They are results driven, willing to take on responsibility, unimpressed with authority, will challenge others, eager to learn		Only know change. Want to help initiate change and will usually do what is asked of them as it's seen as being positive and going with the flow
Technical	Still learning technology, skeptical about using technology, not fond can even be afraid of social media or anything online, e.g. no online banking	Like online courses, thinks they are up to par on technology however it's developing faster than Gen X & Y can keep up. Like to be called at work not at home. Still use email more than other methods of technology		Amazing. Always want to be part of the new thing being released, understand the ins and outs of technology quickly, more resourceful to figure out technology on their own, do not know spelling or grammar due to technology, emojis and social media, which restricts length of messages

Skills	Baby Boomer 1946–1964	Gen X 1965-1976	Gen Y Millenials 1977–1995	Gen Z 1996–Now
Collaboration	Not necessarily opposed, however may feel awkward, could even feel like they are being replaced with younger workers, good team players, anxious to please	Prefer teamwork than individual. When working on a team like to ensure everyone does their share, encourage creativity, flexibility, they work with you not for you, will do a good job when provided with right tools		It's the only way to work. Do not know anything different. It's about enjoying the environment and focus on each other's strengths, highly creative, can also have a 'me first' attitude, open to new ideas, like to take time to hear everyone's ideas. sometimes sharing is more important than the task, want to please others, want to work with friends

Skills	Baby Boomer 1946–1964	Gen X 1965-1976	Gen Y Millenials 1977-1995	Gen Z 1996–Now
Other	Generally very loyal, strong work ethic as it's part of their identity, want to be known as a good worker, careers define them, live to work, believe in political correctness. Expect to be valued in the workplace, don't take criticism well, take things personally	Want independence in the workplace, allow them to have fun, give them time to do things that interest them, liked to be shown their value by getting time off, like continuous learning, it enhances versatility in market, revolt to micro management and question authority, work to live, want to get paid to do a job, prefer balance, look for meaningful work, want to get in, get the work done and move on		Want to contribute to the world, will not put in extra time at work as more important things to do, motivated by learning, short attention span, mentoring is important, obsessed with career development, believe more skills matter hence stay in roles for short period of time, have a more relaxed approach, which can be perceived as disrespectful to other generations

As you see, everyone brings traits to the table, the key is to recognize each other's strengths and build on those. With respect to each other's opportunities accept them. The sooner you do, the easier life will be.

Retention and Measurement

Retention:

Once you have trained your employees, whether it was onboarding, on the job or perhaps areas for career development, what practice do you have in place to measure the employee's learning to ensure they have retained what they have been taught? The general rule is to apply what you have learned, however if this is not done right away and the employees solely took notes or maybe just listened to a training session why would you pay them to attend/obtain training? Incorporating a training retention plan not only makes good business sense, it's also beneficial to your employee and their development. Remember, you are investing in your employee, therefore you care and because you also expect a return on investment, therefore do not leave the retention plan up to the employee.

<u>On average, people remember</u>
10% of what they read
20% of what they hear
30% of what they see
50% of what they see and hear
70% of what they say and write
90% of what they do

<u>On average, people forget</u>
50% of information within one hour
70% of the information within 24 hours
90% of information within a week

After any training session, you should have a 30-60 minute recap powwow. This powwow is intended to highlight the material and connect it to the business or task at hand. For example: You and your team attended a leadership training on how to give recognition and suggestions for improvement to fellow colleagues. Very few people will actually use the material they just learned as they won't believe they will need it or will most likely be scared to deliver part of the message. Therefore, after your training session you ask everyone to come to the board meeting where they have to test out their new skills. Each employee gets partnered up with a fellow colleague, and they have to follow through with giving each other recognition and suggested improvement. You do not only do it once, you get people to do this four, five maybe even six times. The more frequently someone is "forced" to do the task the more comfortable they will feel. Your ultimate goal is to get your employees and yourself to make an emotional connection with the task as this will help trigger a memory. Once the task is a memory you can search for that memory when needed. It is much easier to search for a memory in one's mind than it is to search for a perceived feeling and/or something you never actually experienced.

Sometimes you also have only one or two employees attend a training session and it's those employees' responsibility to transfer knowledge. If this is the case, you would task those employees to take notes on important points relevant to the role and business perhaps bring back material to share with others and ensure you organize a transfer of knowledge session within the day of someone attending a session. Why am I specific on what notes to take? If you just advise someone to take notes, they will not listen to the training and simply write everything down. By only writing and not processing, the information that they write will be lost in translation as they will not be able to make the connection to the purpose of the material. Many training sessions these days provide relevant notes at the end of the session as a recap, or cheat sheet so that participants can give the trainer their full attention.

Measurement:

The best way to see if your employees are applying what they have learned is through their day to day practices. Pay attention to their behaviour, the way they are now performing such a task or collaborating with others. When a new best practice is embedded into someone's life it becomes a new norm. You will see and hear other's comment on how Brad seems to have "grown up" and/or is more communicative than before. These are cues you are looking for to assess if the training is effective.

You can also review someone's performance through their annual performance review, tie in an aspect of training and development to someone's bonus and also ask the employee to conduct a self- assessment of what they have learned and how they are applying it.

Reward:

To foster a continuous learning environment, employees should also be rewarded for applying and sharing what they have learned. These rewards do not necessarily need to be monetary. I have seen communal areas where employers display designation/course certificates as a method to show their appreciation. A few examples are: You could give your employees opportunities for time off or a preferred parking spot. We will go into reward and recognition in more detail in the Employee Engagement section.

Training and Development Takeaways

- ✓ Invest in your people; when you invest in them they will invest in you
- ✓ Be the leader and continuously coach and check in with your employees; do not expect them to approach you
- ✓ Create T&D plans for all areas of your business such as onboarding, required training, self-development, career development, operational considerations such as generational differences.
- ✓ Understand and appreciate that everyone learns differently, and this is not a time when you can have a one size fits all approach

✓ Have a training retention plan in place to ensure your employees apply what they have learned, and you are getting a return on your investment

Employee Engagement

I always wondered what employee engagement meant when I was a regular employee and not part of human resources. Besides the definition of keeping employees happy, why did businesses have such a focus on engagement? For the first 7–8 years of my adult life I mostly worked for medium to large-sized companies, which conducted surveys every year to measure employee engagement. These surveys asked personal questions such as my position, years of service, if I was male or female, my age group, etc. Then, the majority of the actual questions were about the company, the leadership, and the overall environment. So many people always talked about how uncomfortable they felt answering these surveys, they were doubtful that the responses were anonymous especially when people could be narrowed down by demographics. If the survey was written by hand, then yes perhaps your leader would recognize your writing, or if you used expressions, words or even told the same story you have told people before then your leader may know it was you.

I may not be the typical employee, yet if you are asking me for my opinion I will give you my opinion whether it was on a survey or in person. I may not have a fear of retaliation as others seem to have because I have a different outlook. I believe engagement surveys give people a chance to be honest, respectful and help not only ourselves to grow and develop yet also the company and leadership team. When people are too shy to speak up and just agree with everything there is no opportunity for growth. If a company is not willing to grow we will see if that company still exists in 15–20 years. Adapting to the market and to the needs of employees is how a business stays competitive because employees truly are a business's best asset. When employees complain around the water cooler, or at lunch breaks about the company, what good does that do? When someone goes home and continues to complain to their partner about work, express how unhappy they are, how they don't like so and so. WHAT IS THE POINT? When people bring this negativity and unaccountable behaviour home it affects everyone at home as well. Why are these types of people getting up every day going to work for a company with people they don't like? Why are they wasting their lives being unhappy?

I am and have always been a very direct person. When someone is complaining to me, I listen to a certain point. Then, I have always responded with something such as, "Do something about it." If you are so unhappy don't just tell people, take accountability and take charge. As we grow up we have responsibilities, families to care for, bills to pay and want a certain lifestyle. Okay yes, I absolutely agree, I too have all those things. However, if you don't like your job are you prepared to feel like you are in jail for 40–50 years of your life? So you either speak up on your engagement surveys, speak directly to your leader or you suck it up. You need to stop bitching and complaining and keep your current job, or quit and find something you love to do which will bring you joy, happiness with a paycheque. The rebuttal I get to this is always, "It's not that easy". Well, no it's not. If you make it complicated it will be complicated.

For over 15 years being part of HR, I feel that measuring employee engagement is just as important as I felt in my early teens. It is an opportunity to give your employees a voice, allow employees to share their insights, a chance for people to speak up, share their ideas, beliefs and if all is well, thank their leaders and employers for being part of the team. The difference now is that I understand why certain questions are asked, how to read results and what to do with them. In this section we will cover employee surveys, options for companies that do not have formal surveys, employee recognition and other tips and suggestions on how to keep your employees engaged.

———

All leaders within the company must be dedicated to their employees in order to achieve the highest engagement ...

———

Story Time:

Engagement has become a common word in the workplaces of today. Some of the common phrases around engagement one may hear are "he is very engaged in his project" or "she has an engaging approach with her team" or maybe even "their culture is very engaging". So what is Employee Engagement? It is when your workplace captures the hearts and minds of the employees. The employees are passionate about their roles and are committed to the organization and their success while giving discretionary effort in all areas of their work. Employees who are truly engaged with their roles, leaders and their company have reduced turnover, higher productivity and efficiencies, which equate to increased profit and higher customer satisfaction for the company.

All leaders within the company must be dedicated to their employees in order to achieve the highest engagement. There are many ways to engage your employees, but it starts with transparent two-way communication, development feedback, career advancement opportunities, learning and development opportunities, cultural diversity and inclusivity, fair practices and equal compensation, benefits and incentives, recognition, flexible hours of work, and creating an autonomous work environment. Leaders who dedicate themselves to these engagement drivers and create a trusted and inclusive work environment set themselves up for success! Leaders who drive engagement within their business must also live it themselves and always be authentic. Engaged employees are bred from authentic leaders.

A leader allows the voices of the employees to be heard. When participating in Engagement Surveys in the workplace this gives you measurable data that you can review, evaluate and action.

Remember that Engagement Survey results tell you the internal tone of your culture. The measurement of the answers is scientifically weighed based on the responses of your people. You never want to influence a result by coaching employees on how to answer. Doing this not only shows lack of leadership but it also shows the employees that they do not really have a voice and you are not interested in the value of an authentic and positive culture.

Story Time:

About eight years ago, I was working with one of my locations to review their action plan derived from the Annual Engagement Survey. This location struggled with lasting leadership as there was a new leader every year for a four-year span. The results of their Engagement Survey were poor for four years as well. The average Engagement over the four years was about 28 per cent and the District Engagement was 78 per cent while the National Engagement was 72 per cent. I developed a plan to find great leadership who would dedicate themselves to the business and the employees. Once

I found the person that I believed would be a great leader for this location I sat with them to review the Engagement Results and asked them to develop an action plan for this location with what they felt were the core concerns driving the disengagement.

Her plan was more detailed than I had seen before from any location and she had detailed out what she felt was needed. She then met with all of the employees to hear their concerns over the last four years in the business and added a couple more points to her action plan. She dedicated her leadership to working this action plan for the people and with the people. She showed vulnerability and commitment throughout the next year with regular meetings and follow up. She put processes into place that were never there before. She cleaned up their associate rest area and promoted positive messaging and communication boards. She allowed monthly learning and development sessions for each team. She created Individual Development Plans for those who wanted to move up in the business with a clear plan on how to get there. She taught managers how to manage and lead with high ethics and morals.

She took every engagement driver she learned from the Engagement results and wove it into the culture of the business. She allowed people to fail and learn from their failures the opportunities they needed to master. She created a highly productive workforce that all wanted the business and themselves and their colleagues to succeed. She led by showing empathy, compassion and drive for results. Within 10 months of her coming into the store they once again had an Engagement Survey and this time the results spoke for themselves with 88 per cent – a 60 per cent improvement within a ten-month time frame of dedicated leadership. She learnt from mistakes and kept going. She showed them what ownership and accountability was. She was an Authentic Leader.

Karla

18 Years in HR

Canada

Engagement Surveys

"Employee engagement illustrates the commitment and energy that employees bring to work and is a key indicator of their involvement and dedication to the organization. Employees who are engaged are more productive, content and more likely to be loyal to an organization." —Human Resources Council

"Employee engagement is the emotional commitment the employee has to the organization and its goals. This emotional commitment means engaged employees actually care about their work and their company."

—Kevin Kruse, *Forbes*

Engagement surveys are one way to measure your employees' engagement. The purpose of the survey is to ensure there is trust between both you and the employee, through communication, respect and fairness. They are usually conducted annually to see what motivates your employees, recognition, pay, development and leadership relationships. If you have a budget for engagement, I would recommend a company that specializes in measuring engagement. You can do a Google search, or perhaps you are familiar with some companies within your own country such as Qualtrics. com, Gallup.com, officevibe.com, tinypulse.com, surveymonkey.com, quantumworkplace.com, deloitte.com, and many others. Costs can range from a few thousand on SurveyMonkey as it is more of a do it yourself to over six figures depending on your size of staff and the company and services you hire to administer the survey. Either way, measuring engagement is important. Since you are investing in your company by having employees, you are paying those employees to fulfill their job descriptions and hopefully more, it is wise to keep a continuous watch on the environment in your workplace. If this is your first time measuring engagement and you have a staff count of 100 or less, I would suggest to start small and easy.

A: Choose your survey provider

On SurveyMonkey, you can have a short 10-question survey for free. There are no demographic questions, just an introductory note to advise the employee of the purpose of conducting the survey, and then a thank you note for participating, which you can alter yourself. If you would like more than 10 questions you can pay a small fee to have full access to the site and different reporting methods. As noted above, you can also choose a more robust company that specializes in measuring employee engagement. For this example we will continue with a small survey on SurveyMonkey.

B: Create your questions

There are many categories for you to consider when creating your survey. Employee satisfaction, their commitment to your business, teamwork and collaboration, customer interactions, career and skill development, trust and respect, reward and recognition, leadership effectiveness and so on. If you are going to narrow it down to 10 questions, I suggest choosing categories that have the biggest impact on your business such as Collaboration and Teamwork, Trust and Respect, Communication, Rewards and Recognition,

Customer Interaction, Career and Skill Development, Leadership, overall Employee Satisfaction. You can also use an easy scale of 1-5; 1 representing unsatisfactory and 5 representing excellent. Or, you can choose the words only for your employees to use to describe their answers.

1. The people I work with cooperate to reach our common goals (Collaboration)

2. I am treated with dignity and respect (Trust and Respect)

3. There is good teamwork and cooperation between departments (Teamwork)

4. I receive the information and communication I need to do my job effectively (Communication)

5. I regularly receive appropriate recognition when I do a good job (Rewards and Recognition)

6. Customer problems and concerns are dealt with quickly (Customer Interactions)

7. My department has a clear understanding of our customers' needs (Customer Interactions)

8. The person I report to supports my ongoing learning and development (Career and Skill development)

9. What more can we do to improve the working climate at "your company name" (Open-ended - Satisfaction)

10. Any additional suggestions or comments? (Open-ended comments)

I have had people ask me why use two of the 10 questions related to customers. Well, without customers your business would not exist. Therefore, as they are the bread and butter of your business it makes good business sense to ensure your employees interact well and are serving your clients appropriately. If you choose to have a longer survey you would ask 4–5 questions in each category and perhaps you could add a few more categories, such as safety / security / wellness, plus subjects specific to your business only like scheduling, breaks, performance reviews, etc.

C: Introduce the idea

Draft an introductory letter you will share with all staff. Make it personal, not a typical template document. Employees need to know it's coming from you and it is in your words. Talk to your employees in person about this initiative, add the letter to employee paystubs to ensure everyone gets a copy; if that is not possible you can add it to a communication binder and have a method for everyone to date and sign that they have read the letter. An example of what you can create is:

In an effort to continuously improve our business and overall environment, we will be conducting an employee engagement survey to obtain your feedback to assist us in staying on track with our company values, support you in the workplace and ensure you are valued in the business. Your honest and open participation is essential to helping us understand what is working and what is not.

You will receive the link to complete the survey via your email address and will have 10 days to complete the survey between (insert date) and (insert date). Your answers will not be shared with others, they will be read by (insert leader name or outside HR organization) only. Collective results with be posted in the lunch room on (insert date), (which is about five business days after the last day to answer). We will then have an engagement committee, one representative per department to assist with our action plan and future engagement of the company. If you wish to volunteer for the committee, please see your immediate leader.

Thank you for your collaboration. I look forward to providing you with a rewarding and fun workplace.

D: <u>Analyze your results</u>

Once your results are ready, writing a thank you note to staff is appreciative. Something similar to what is above, thanking them for the open and honest feedback, and introducing the idea of an engagement team. Explain that management and staff will have the chance to review and action the results. You can also ask for volunteers or you can appoint an engagement team, whichever works for you. Do not shy away from having an employee who tends to be negative on an engagement team, this can be an opportunity to enlighten this employee and get them to focus their energy on something good. Just remember to be transparent and include your next steps of the process on this Thank You Note. You can post the Thank You note in your lunch room with a synopsis copy of your results; this way everyone gets to see it. The analytical area is crucial to the success of your employee engagement. I have personally worked for companies that were very poor at sharing, analyzing and actioning results then all employees including myself feel "what is the point", why go to all this effort to ask me for feedback and then do nothing with it? Do not be one of these employers. There are two parts to analyzing your data. There is yourselves between management and also with your staff. I recommend doing both. It does not need to take long.

JLP Tip: Have an engagement committee and include only a middle manager not senior manager to create a stronger comfort level. Choose items that employees can focus on, things that are within their control.

Management: Depending on your survey format, you can choose to provide everyone with a synopsis and/or share the raw data. Sharing raw data creates a more authentic work environment, yet if you choose to go this method do speak to your leaders beforehand so they know this is for information purposes only and not to be used as retaliation, or for a witch hunt to find out exactly who said what, etc. This may seem childish to say, however I have personally witnessed many negative situations with leaders receiving their data whether it has been filtered or not.

HR Jail: I worked for a company that had an agreement with the survey provider that the survey results would be filtered and shared to department heads. I was in HR at the time, therefore myself and only a few other senior leaders received the raw data. One year, the survey provider made a mistake and sent the raw data to all department heads including myself and the senior leaders. For the first few days no one thought there was anything different because I and the senior leadership team received the results in the same fashion as we had for many years. One Friday morning I got a visit from an employee (Alan) who as very upset, he was almost crying. He wanted to quit. Alan explained to me that his direct leader Jeff questioned him and others in the department about survey results as he wanted to know who had said what. It seemed Jeff was called an asshole in the survey and Jeff was taking this personally.
I and the leadership team quickly realized the mistake the survey provider had made, and we held a team meeting with all managers. Since we were Day 3 by that point, we were not sure who had

read the results or who had access to them. We had over 75 people attend the meeting: department heads and their direct reports who were middle managers. There was nothing we could do but explain it was a mistake. However, now that the data were released we had to come up with a plan. We continued with our engagement action plan, held committees and for the most part there was very little damage control to do, except for Jeff and his department. We held a separate meeting for Jeff and the department.

Openly discussing what we had heard, Jeff admitted to asking around for information, yet he said he was genuinely wanting to know what he could do better. He didn't want anyone to feel or think he was an asshole, which is when I spilled the beans in front of everyone. "Jeff you have been called worse than an asshole for four years you just did not know it. There is nothing wrong with this as someone is expressing their feelings and that is the purpose of having a survey." Jeff was shocked, yet it was also a wakeup call to him. Jeff now made it his mission to help support all members of his team to ensure no one felt left out or that he was unkind in any way. He personally met with all his staff, apologized individually and asked for one-on-one feedback on what he could do better. Within three months, Jeff's department was rocking it. Customers raved about Jeff, his staff and always wanted to come back to be served by them. In this situation, Jeff and his organization worked out favourably yet it does not always work that way.

> » Never speak to employees about what they specifically said on a survey, or ask direct questions. The only time you can do this if an employee signed the comment they wrote or if they provided you with the comment in person. You can

lose trust very quickly as a leader and it takes forever and sometimes never to get it back

» Foster an open environment with employee surveys. They are a chance for people to share their thoughts and feelings

» Understand as a leader it is your role to take the high road at all times

Engagement committees work well as you are getting your staff involved in the analysis and actions to help maintain or improve the results. You have to ensure you are not "dumping" the analysis and action plan onto your staff, this is a collaborative effort. A good rule of thumb is to have one person per department with one middle manager yet no senior leadership. The middle manager will allow the team to ask questions about procedures and policies and still make the engagement team feel comfortable to bring up issues. The team will need to have 3–4 meetings throughout the year.

#1. The first meeting will be their introductory and brainstorming session and should be about one hour and it is a paid meeting. Have the manager take notes and keep things brief. They will read the survey, and decide what areas to focus on. You can also get a head start by deciding the areas to work on with your management team, thus providing the engagement team with already suggested topics. When looking at areas to focus on, also do not only focus on opportunities. This is frequently a human reaction, to look at what is wrong and come up with a plan to fix it. You want to have a good ratio of things to improve and things to maintain. Why things to maintain? Well, if you are scored well on them, your staff evidently like what you are doing related to that topic so you want to ensure you keep it up. In the end you will have anywhere from 3–6 items to include in your action plan.

It is also not recommended to focus solely on specific questions, think more about what category the question fits into. For example, if you choose the question"I regularly receive appropriate recognition when I do a good job", this question fits into a Rewards and Recognition category. So there is two things to consider; # 1 The question has an "I" in it andwhen you go around the room and ask the engagement committee if they have had any personal issues with recognition, they will say all is fine. In this case instead ask the engagement committee how is recognition in our department and within our organization? This will help get the engagement team to think more globally. Things are always up to someone's perception and if you keep this too specific it may not apply, so this is one of those times in HR where you should think more generally as opposed to specific individuals.

What does an action plan look like?

Item for review or to maintain	Actions to be taken	Who is responsible	Timeline	Notes, dates when completed and/or part of best practices
#1 Team work	Engagement team to promote cross training and lunch with employees from different departments	All members of the engagement team	Revisit in 45 days	Target date 3 months

Item for review or to maintain	Actions to be taken	Who is responsible	Timeline	Notes, dates when completed and/or part of best practices
# 2 Recognition	All leaders to recognize one staff member of a different department each week, staff to recognize each other	Leaders and all staff	Review it weekly if the goal is weekly at weekly management team meetings.	Should be ongoing

E: <u>Implement</u>

Once the plan is decided, the senior leadership will have the final approval and then the action plan is put into place. The engagement team will decide who is working on what, or perhaps everyone has a part to play with each area of the action plan. Whatever is decided is now part of simple change management: incorporating the new suggestions into the department's/company's best practices so they become the new norm.

#2: The second, third and fourth meetings, which are about 45–60 days apart are updates on the implementation. The manager will ask questions on what is working and what is not and document those as well. Each of these meetings should be 45 minutes or less. You can even share the notes from these meetings with the rest of your staff so they see the progress the engagement team is achieving. Add them to the report and thank you note in the lunch room perhaps.

———

Pay special attention to new staff who were hired after last year's survey.

———

Once the engagement team has had their fourth meeting, it is usually about 60 days out before doing your next annual survey. To ensure you are well prepared, review the results and action plans with current staff and pay special attention to new staff who were hired after last year's survey. The new staff would not be aware of what took place prior to them joining so instead of having them go into a survey blind, let them know what the survey was, its purpose, who is on the engagement team and what was done from last year to now.

Measuring Employee Engagement without formal surveys

There are many companies who never have and/or do not want to conduct surveys. If you are one of those, what can you do to measure engagement? As noted earlier, your employees are your biggest asset so you should at least do something.

Quarterly / Bi-Yearly One-on-Ones:

We already know the importance of obtaining direct feedback from your employees, this method can be quick and help build interpersonal relationships. Let's say you have 45 employees. If you have a 15-minute check-in with each employee, that is approximately 11-12 hours of time it would take you to have an open discussion with your employees. For one day and half, it is worth it. You would need to schedule everyone during the same time period and block off your calendar. You should also have an introductory letter similar to the engagement survey letter. You would ask every single employee the same questions and document their answers so that you can go back and answer things if you can't on the spot and also provide a tally of the results to staff.

1. Describe the atmosphere at work for me.
2. What do you like about working here?
3. What would you like to change about working here?
4. Do you feel comfortable speaking to management or myself about any questions or concerns?
5. Is there anything additional you would like to add?

Keeping this short and sweet is important to be effective and allows you to do it more frequently. The more often you do this, the more open the communication will be in your business as people will not wait for their quarterly one-on-one; they will feel open to ask questions and speak up at any time. You can tailor your questions as the year progresses, yet always ask everyone the same questions. People will talk, compare notes after and you want to eliminate the possibility of perceived favouritism. Asking the same questions helps ensure your process is fair.

————

Remember! Always ask everyone the same questions.

————

Again at the end of this process you would include a Thank You note with a recap of the results for staff. If you do not share what you have learned you will create gossip, anxiety and too many unanswered questions. The note below takes 15 minutes to write and becomes a part of fostering a positive work environment for your staff.

Thank you for attending our quarterly one-on-ones. All employees were able to participate. In this quarter's results we obtained the following feedback:

1. *Over 80% of you enjoy the work environment.*

2. *The people, the location, the camaraderie and being part of our organization are the common things you like about working here.*

3. *Many people spoke about the parking and/or the lack thereof. As we are a downtown location, parking is scarce, however I will speak to some parking lot management companies and get back to you by (insert date).*

4. *We seem to often run out of vanilla coffee for our machine and the bathrooms are not getting cleaned as often. We will look into this and come up with a solution by (insert date).*

5. *Everyone felt comfortable coming to us with any questions and concerns. This has made me feel very proud and humbled and I thank you for creating and being part of this wonderful organization.*

Thank you again and please do not hesitate to come to me or any member of management. We look forward to continuing to grow and expand as a company with all of your knowledge and expertise.

Other Options:

A. Paper questionnaire

Similar to the 10 questions on SurveyMonkey, you could have a PDF version, pass it around and have a communal place where people can leave their completed results. Usually the drop-off place should be an area that all employees use and/or walk by to help your employees feel comfortable. You would also give employees a specific amount of time to complete the paper survey and then follow a similar plan to analyze, share, and implement an action plan.

B. On-Line quick 2 minutes weekly questionnaire

A company like Officevibe has a free plan then a USD$4.00 per user per month. For your staff of 45 that is about $180 per month, and $2,160 per year. It is a survey sent to each individual email address. This is a minimal fee to spend to help measure your employee engagement. The service is five questions every week and it takes about two minutes to complete. The leader receives a variety of options on reports for the results, which you can share with the team. This type of system also helps you track trends, which is beneficial to the growth of your business.

C. Suggestion Box:

There are many pros and cons to suggestion boxes. I have seen them work well and other times disasters. A few golden suggestions are:

- Keep the box in a communal place where everyone goes or has access to, like a lunch room

- Lock the box and/or ensure no one can put their hands in to take anything out to read and put back.

- Every suggestion must be addressed. You should have a small communication board or binder that is connected to the box and when a suggestion comes in you document the date, say thank you for providing this suggestion and write what the result/action is. Even if you can't do something about the suggestion you still write that you can't do something about it and explain why.

- Refresh. Do not just leave the box there indefinitely. It needs to create interest and exclusivity. For example, have a specific two weeks every quarter where you have the box open. If you have it there indefinitely it will be something you need to continuously manage and it will eventually become a garbage box and something for employees to complain about.

Recognition

This is one of my favourite parts of human resources and overall business environments: finding ways to appreciate your employees, say thank you for their achievements. Recognition can be public, private or group recognition. It should be continuous and shared with all employees and when individualized it should be personal. Recognition means different things to different people, so you need to get to know your employees so you know how they liked to be recognized. There are so many myths to recognition: it costs too much money, people don't appreciate it, and they become accustomed and expect it. My answer: it all depends on what you offer and how you offer it. Every leader has the amazing ability to create a wonderful work environment; there should be no excuses as to why recognition is not part of one's culture.

Formal Recognition:

Every company should have at least one method of formal recognition. Formal recognition, meaning any employee and/or leader has access to recognize anyone in the company. It is a program run by the company and not created by one department.

✓ It can be an electronic program where someone logs on to an internal company site, completes a form and off goes the Thank You note. The employee receives it by email. There are companies that supply such services, which can be used on mobile devices as well. They usually send the recognition in a form of a certificate. Employees tend to like this as they can print it and add them to their desk, cubicle or locker.

✓ If you are not ready to spend money, you can create your own in-house program. Have a cork board, call it the Recognition Board in a central area and create WOW sticky notes. You can even get some printed at Vistaprint.com for a very nominal fee. Then any employee/leader can write each other a note and leave it on the board. Clean the board once a month and write out all the names of people who got recognized that month on a sheet and post it on the same board. Do not throw out the WOW notes, add them to people's employee files as a method of tracking when you go to conduct someone's performance review.

✓ Every month, or once a quarter you can award something to one or two staff members who were recognized in the past month/quarter. If you have a lot of staff and want to recognize two people per month or per quarter you can include all the WOW cards in a hat and draw one winner then management chooses the other winner. The recognition: a preferred parking spot, or a paid lunch on the day of the employee's choice, maybe they get to leave early on a Friday and get paid for the remainder of the day.

✓ Years of service: When someone has been loyal to your company for 5, 10, 15 and more years you should thank them for it. The most common recognition is a pin someone receives to add to their name tag or badge, sometimes it is a plaque or award. Although it may be great to get a pin or plaque it will be something that gets lost or collects dust at home. I would suggest thinking through your options for awards prior to spending money on something your staff member may not be able to do something with. You could have a pin with a gift card, or certificate with a gift. Years of service awards are very important to people so make them meaningful. Do not provide an electric toothbrush after 10 years of service as this may not be the positive employee engagement you are going for.

✓ Feedback meeting: We will go into more detail in the Performance Management section, however advising people how they are doing and how they fit into the bigger picture is important to self-esteem.

✓ Other: Does your company offer flex hours, financial rewards, cross training opportunities, tuition reimbursement? These can all be seen as forms of recognition.

✓ Social Committee: A group of individuals who will help organize fun events and activities for all employees such as bowling, baby showers, etc. Sometimes there is also social fun where all employees can contribute $2 to the fund every paycheque and the events organized by the social committee are subsidized by this fund. If you choose to have a fund, you should have a signed agreement by all employees that participating in the fund is voluntary and they can stop contributing to the fund at any time by giving the employer 2 weeks' notice. (Two weeks because it is common for employees to be paid every 2 weeks, if this is different then change it according to your business.)

<u>Informal Recognition:</u>

This is everything else you do to say Thank You to your employees:

✓ Verbal individualized and group Thank You messages

✓ Thank you notes, cards

✓ Pizza lunches

✓ Donuts and coffee

- ✓ Birthday cards or special occasion cards
- ✓ Great job, well done
- ✓ Summer BBQs
- ✓ Gift cards, movie passes
- ✓ Christmas dinners
- ✓ Celebrate individual and company milestones

Other Tips and Suggestions

- ✓ Positive employee engagement is for all work environments. When employees have questions or concerns it is important for leaders to own the message and not pass blame on to others. This will show the employee respect and build honesty and trust. Even if a leader does not have the answers to questions, it is the leader's responsibility to find the answer to address the concern.

- ✓ Group feedback sessions can also be useful when you are asking general questions or tackling a specific concern. Such sessions can be administered by management, or an outside HR employee or consultant. Whoever is running the session needs to be comfortable receiving feedback and controlling the meeting to ensure it does not become a "bitch session".

- ✓ HAVE FUN: Allow your employees to laugh, engage with each other. Encourage them to take lunch together. Building relationships with fellow colleagues increases loyalty, retention, and general happiness at work.

- ✓ Engage in open feedback frequently. You do not need to wait for surveys, performance reviews and/or formal feedback sessions. One of the top five things that all employees have said in my experience over the past 15+ years in human resources is they would like more feedback. People want to hear from their leaders, they want to know "where they stand", how they are doing, and what can they improve. Engaging in feedback is great for overall engagement.

✓ Be authentic: leaders are human, they make mistakes, have a bad day and may not know all aspects of a business. If something goes wrong, or when a leader makes a mistake, apologize to staff, let them know you will fix the concern, tell them you are sorry you let them down. Employees will appreciate your honesty and have a closer connection to you than if you cover something up or not address it at all.

Why Employee Engagement is Important to Every Business

The diagram below sums up how positive employee engagement affects all aspects of a business.

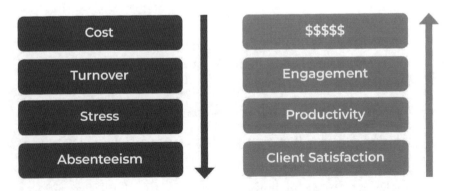

Employee Engagement Takeaways

✓ Keeping your employees happy, measuring their engagement is key to the success of your business.

✓ Foster a positive and open communication environment.

✓ Leadership needs to understand and execute their responsibilities, lead by example.

✓ Find an engagement model that is right for you, and/or combine a few (Surveys, One-on-Ones, Feedback sessions).

✓ Ensure you have a recognition program in place, both formal and informal. Try to change things up with the informal and when giving individual recognition, personalize it.

✓ Make your workplace fun.

CHAPTER 5

PERFORMANCE MANAGEMENT

YOU'RE FIRED! This seems to be the misconception of the purpose of performance management. I am of the belief that leaders have a role to play when someone is not performing. It can be due to a lack of training, coaching, perhaps even a lack of reward and recognition from the leader. There are certainly situations where employees get off track for personal reasons, and the goal is to bring the employee back on track, improve their performance, improve productivity, and overall effectiveness. Another misconception is that performance management is an extension of performance assessments, also called performance reviews.

When someone is not performing well at work, as a leader you address these issues during a performance appraisal meeting yet this is not performance management. The document you use during a performance appraisal includes a variety of other metrics, responsibilities as demonstrated in the section below. The documents you use for performance management we will review in further detail during this chapter. So why is it important to have an effective performance management process?

✓ Employees receive clear direction, they can be more focused on their career development, and have an increase in their job satisfaction.

✓ Organizations will get more productivity from employees, align employees with business goals, and reduce turnover and absenteeism.

Have you ever had a job where a fellow colleague comes in late frequently, does not pull their weight and seems to get away with it? You have tried to help out that colleague, offered to switch shifts, help divide workload and your efforts do not seem to be working? Have you also asked your boss, other colleagues have asked your boss, and still no changes? You genuinely want to help this person and at the same time you don't want to feel that you are being taken advantage of; you want to be part of a business that treats people fairly. This is just one of the many examples as to why performance management exists. It is an opportunity to help someone perform, guide them to meet the standards required to do their job. When one, two or even three employees are not performing in a workplace it takes a toll on everyone else. Other employees feel used, devalued and start to get a bad impression of the leader and organization.

When someone is consistently late should they be fired? Does being late over and over warrant losing your job? Usually the answer is no – being late warrants being performance managed. During a performance management process there could be times it does not end positively, and someone gets terminated. However, this is not the main purpose of performance management. Performance Management is a process that is meant to help an employee 'get back on track'. We all have times in our lives where we need a little more guidance than usual, perhaps we become too complacent, or something has happened in our personal lives that changes our focus and unfortunately affects our performance. We all need to realize shit happens and it is okay. No one is perfect, and no one should be expected to be perfect, yet all employees should meet expectations with respect to performance.

I find it interesting when I meet someone and tell them I am in HR and they always want to share a story with me about a time when they "pulled" someone into the office. These are usually stories where someone is being performance managed. It is leaders like this who use this process and give it a negative perception. Why on earth must someone be so disrespected and say "I pulled Suzie into the office", or when leaders say to me "You should have seen the look on her face". No human being should be treated this way, no matter what the offence. As a leader, every employee deserves to be treated with respect. I have investigated and terminated many people over my years in HR, some are even my friends; friends I am still in contact with and care deeply about. Of course they were not happy with me at the time, however they are the ones that made the mistake, not me. I was just the messenger, doing my job. In the end a leader must choose their words carefully.

Now, let's dive into performance management and all its components. In this chapter we will review performance assessments, the progressive discipline process, the difference between types of performance management and employee exiting. As you read this section, remember your goal as leaders is to set someone up for success. If someone gets off the train at the wrong stop, help them get back on that train until they are ready to get off at the appropriate stop.

Performance Assessments

While a performance appraisal is typically done yearly, some organizations have them bi-yearly. They are meant to provide feedback to an employee about their overall performance by identifying training, coaching, or mentoring opportunities. They are also usually connected to compensation. When an employee is meeting expectations or exceeding expectations that employee should be compensated accordingly. All areas of an employee's performance must be measured, both hard and soft skills. A hard skill is an objective – something specific, teachable, technical, or administrative. A soft skill is subjective – personal qualities, habits, attitudes.

Many companies will follow a general rule of thumb when it comes to setting goals and standards. One example of this is called the SMART objectives, also sometimes referred to the START objectives.

S = Specific
M = Measurable or T = Tangible
A = Acceptable
R = Realistic
T = Time bound

In your organization you can use the same objectives listed above or you can create your own.

1. How to identify your performance goals and standards.

✓ Review the job descriptions you created and use those skills and abilities to create "hard skills" performance standards. These standards will be more specific to one's individual job.

✓ Review the company objectives and add those to someone's performance standards. Be careful not to include too many things an employee has no control over. For example, a senior executive will have a higher ability to influence labour hours as they are part of creating a budget, scheduling employees. An employee can influence labour hours it by coming in on time, not incurring overtime, etc.

✓ Review the job descriptions again, not just one individual's job description but a combination of all positions. First, separate them by department, then compare by the whole organization. You are looking to create consistency between roles, departments, and the total business. Soft skills help define your culture, therefore most if not all employees should have similar soft skills traits (communication, leadership, adaptability, teamwork, time management, willingness to learn).

✓ Do not forget your clients. It may already be part of your hard or soft skills standards, yet if it is not there it is recommended to include something related to client satisfaction, client relationships, client retention.

✓ Lastly, you will have an area for the flavour of the year. Something your company is focusing on, a new initiative, perhaps a department goal, which may vary based on market needs, change management, etc.

The board of directors or CEO will review and decide the company's objectives and this will trickle down to each employee, being slightly tailored to each individual role. In the end, your company's performance goals and standards should coordinate across departments as well as the whole organization. It is wise if the goals are always Specific, Measurable, Acceptable, Realistic with defined timelines.

2. How to define performance measurements

I suggest to use a simple rating system, described in A, B, or C.

Style	1	2	3	4	5	6
A	Not Meeting Standards	Below Standards	Meeting Standards	Slightly Above Standards	Exceeding Standards	N/A
B	Poor	Fair	Acceptable	Good	Excellent	N/A
C	Unsatisfactory	Marginal	Satisfactory	Good	Very Good	Outstanding

To ensure all leaders use the rating system appropriately you also need to define what your style means. Perhaps even give examples. This will help when you are having a discussion with your employee to explain to them why they have been rated a 3, and not 4. We will use style B as an example

Rating	1	2	3	4	5
	Poor	Fair	Acceptable	Good	Excellent
Description	Not meeting goals / having troubles with other colleagues / receiving client complaints	Needs a lot of supervision about goals / a few employee complaints / concerns with client retention	Meeting goals / gets along with colleagues / receives positive client comments on occasion	Achieves goals with confidence / team oriented / increased client retention	Over achiever, additional work provided / leading team projects / clients ask for the employee by name

You can add as much descriptive information as you see fit for each performance rating. Every time a performance assessment is being conducted, it would be wise for the leader to have this performance rating description readily available to help them decide where an employee fits and also share the performance rating with employees. It's important for the process and the employee themselves to know and feel they are being assessed fairly and not by a leader's impressions. Having a structure helps with this. On a side note, you would not measure your hard skills and soft skills in the same sections. Your hard skills are tactical, the soft skills are perceptions / impressions.

3. Decide on your employee assessment approach

A: Leadership assessment – This is a top down approach when only the leader assesses the employee's performance. Sometimes the employee will have an opportunity to discuss/ negotiate yet the final decision is made by the leader.

B: 360° assessment – An employee's performance is assessed by the leader, other colleagues, clients and their own self-assessment.

C: Self-review, then leadership assessment – A leader provides a blank assessment to their employee. The employee has a specific amount of time to review and rate themselves. Once they attend the performance assessment meeting, the leader would have also done his/her own assessment and the final decision is communal – a collaboration and combination of both employee and leader. This is a recommended practice to foster an open, honest feedback session.

4. Create your own performance assessment document
If you are not fond of the above provided suggestions you can create your own. Use a format you are comfortable with (Word, Excel, PowerPoint) and something that all leaders can use easily and have access to on their computers. You could include a mix of hard skills

and soft skills, things that are important to your organization. I also suggest getting a few different people's inputs, perhaps even a focus group with a mix of employee and leaders so that there is full participation and acceptance of your new program. Giving employees the possibility of input helps with promoting the new document and smooths things over if you had an old document you are now wanting to replace. It's part of change management.

See a sample assessment below created in an Excel document. This one is very simple with a 1-5 rating scale, assuming 1 would be unsatisfactory and 5 is excellent. Your assessments will most likely be more robust.

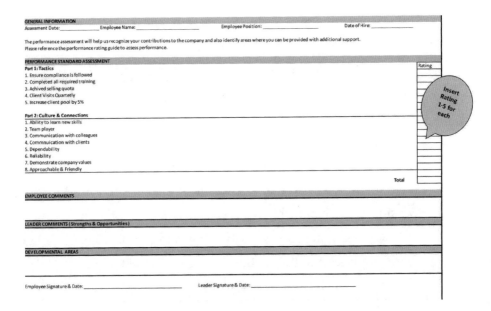

5. Filling out the assessment form

When you have chosen the type of document you will use, then comes the time for the leaders to fill in the information. As noted previously, many companies complete performance assessments annually, however that seems to be changing. With the newer generation in the workforce, people want more frequent and timely feedback, therefore I would suggest having this process quarterly. To complete the actual form usually takes on average 30–45 minutes. To make it easier for you, I suggest saving it on your computer under the employee's name and year (e.g. Josée LP 2019). You should also be cognizant if other people have access to your computer; if they do not then the simple name and year format will work. If you share a computer with others then I suggest creating an encrypted file so the information stays confidential out of respect for your team and each individual employee as well as conforming with privacy laws.

Prior to completing your forms, there are a few things you need to consider. The first is to review your current year's process with respect to performance increases. In many organizations, employees are given a wage/salary increase based on their annual performance assessment, therefore you need to know what your budget is.

Have you decided what assessment approach you are following? No matter which method of documentation you have chosen, if you want to foster an open environment in your workplace you should provide the employee with a blank assessment document a week or so in advance and have them come to your meeting prepared to discuss their performance with you.

One of the most important things is to ensure you take the time to individualize your information. Do not cut and paste comments from one person's document to another. Review the employee's file, take note of all the positive opportunities they had throughout the year. You most likely have notes and recognition on file therefore, consult these prior to doing the assessment. If you are doing an annual assessment, you are evaluating someone's performance for the whole year, not the last few months you can remember. So you need facts from the whole year. (This is also another reason why it may be easier to do assessments quarterly as the employee's current performance is fresh in your mind.)

———

Remember! In many countries, a performance assessment is considered a legal document, therefore take the necessary time to do it right!

———

Be careful on judgement. In the world of HR there is something called "central tendency" where employees get rated in the middle of the scale by default, or the "halo effect" where you allow your rating on one section to bias your ratings for other sections. There is also a strictness and leniency effect where you could be too hard or too soft. Then there is the recency effect when you focus on recent performance. Lastly, there is something called the 'similar to me' bias, which is when you like someone. You feel like they are similar to you so you give them higher ratings. Remember, you have a big responsibility when it comes to completing assessments. This process means a lot to your employees and in many countries, a performance assessment is considered a legal document, therefore take the necessary time to do it right.

Story Time:

In one of my HR roles I supported many department heads during the performance assessment process. I would help leaders with how to fill out the forms, help them understand the rating process and provide tips on having difficult conversations. All employees would obtain their performance assessment at the same time, which would be the end of a person's contract. During my contract, my office was right beside Kesi's who was the head of a large department. Kesi and I got along well, we would meet for lunch, go for a coffee here and there and even bugged each other by knocking on the separating wall of our offices since they were side by side. During one of our coffee breaks, Kesi explained to me his performance process was going to be long this time around as he had many people who were not performing and thus would need to have several difficult conversations with his direct reports.

A few weeks passed during the performance process, and I caught up with Kesi at lunch. I was coming into the mess hall and he was actually leaving, so we stopped in the doorway for a quick chat. I asked him how things were and he started sweating, got all flustered. I decided to skip lunch and walk back to Kesi's office with him. He proceeded to explain to me that he was almost done all his assessments and only had 12 left. I was very happy for him and then was very direct; so why all the emotion. He explained the 12 left were the people who were not performing and he was nervous and losing sleep over having these conversations. Kesi was a tenured leader. It was not the first time he had difficult conversations with people. My reaction is that I started laughing; I laughed so much I even had tears in my eyes. OOOOOOh, Kesi got mad! The look on his face was that of a lion when someone else was eating its prey. He didn't understand why I was laughing. It was not appropriate for me to laugh I know, yet I blurted out to him "You have been torturing yourself for two weeks leaving these difficult conversations for the very end. Have you been doing this every year?"

Kesi was quiet. Then I said, "Why would you not do them at the beginning and get them over and done with so your torture is only a few days instead of a few weeks. Oh my gosh. It was hilarious! Kesi threw a book at me and said, "Okay, Miss Smarty Pants." Luckily, it was a light book and there was no damage and we both continued to laugh. Kesi never left those difficult conversations to the end again. This became an ongoing joke for the years we worked together.

6. The Assessment Meeting

Plan and be prepared – two of the most important words when it comes to performing assessment meetings. Although you have completed formal forms ahead of time, it is wise to review the documents prior to sitting down with the employee so that you know what you will say whether it's positive or negative information. When someone scores low on their assessment, there is a good chance you will be performance managing them, therefore you should not score someone a "meets expectations" and give them a wage increase. These are things we see in HR frequently, employees getting increases while a leader is performing progressive discipline. This is a double standard. Should you end up terminating someone, your labour officers or a judge will be questioning you on your practices. You need to be honest and specific, do not get personal, encourage the employee to talk, and if there are areas for development decide on the plan of action during your meeting.

Having a difficult conversation: When you need to have a difficult conversation with someone the worst thing to do is sugar coat things. If something is not going well, be honest while respecting someone's dignity. An example of a simple process to use is the following: "Bob, when you come in late, other employees need to extend their shift to ensure coverage, which alters people's schedules. Please arrive 10 minutes prior to your shift moving forward. This translates to A: You are explaining the concern B: Explaining what happens because of the concern, and C: Advising of the necessary remedy.

When conducting the performance assessment meeting, two leaders should always be present. A male and female is best to ensure all genders are covered. Anytime for that matter when behind closed doors with an employee discussing performance it is wise to have the employee's immediate supervisor and the department leader or senior leader present for conversations. Why two genders? To avoid discrimination and potentially false accusations. There have been situations where an employee may claim harassment, unfair treatment, etc. if the supervisor and senior leader are of the same gender. It's okay as long as there are two of you. Your first plan is both genders, your backup plan is at least two leaders. What you do not want is just one leader and/or more than two leaders representing the employer as this can be perceived as ganging up on an employee.

If and when you are conducting an investigation or if you have more than one meeting during the same day it is wise to schedule your meetings with at least 15–30 minutes of free time in between to allow you to take notes, take a small break and account for going overtime. Each performance meeting can be 30–60 mins in length. Another reason is not to have employees waiting in line outside your office as they could hear what is being said, and should someone leave your office crying you don't want someone waiting at the door.

Location of the meeting: Your office is most likely the best place, perhaps reserve the conference room if you have one. However, please no coffee shops, no lunch rooms, and no communal areas. (I have seen this happen many times before.) If it is in your office or conference room have a sign on your door so that no one disturbs you, turn your phone off and remove all other distractions out of respect for the employee and the process. The employee is to sit closest to the door so they can leave whenever they want, especially as they may get upset or cry. The ideal setting is to not have a desk in between you and the employee and have your chairs facing each other in a more comfortable setting to be able to observe the employee and read body gestures. If this is not possible, then your backup is the usual office setting.

JLP Tip: Ask your employee to turn their phone off as well and ensure you see the phone being turned off. It is for respect and to avoid the chance of having the meeting recorded without your knowledge.

———

Remember! Be honest and be kind.

———

What happens if the employee does get upset or defensive? Always have tissue in your office, and allow the employee to express their emotions. Denial or anger can happen and as long as the environment is safe, the person may need to blow off steam. Do not over explain your point or ramble. When someone is upset, our human reaction is to feel bad so you may start altering your words or decision, remember be honest and be kind. If the employee keeps pushing for information, you may need to put an end to the conversation. Sometimes, it is best to not say anything and address the issue later once emotions have died down. If you both cannot agree, you can revisit the concern once you both have more time to think about the concern.

After you have explained to the employee the purpose of the write-up, the employee signs the document and then you should give them a copy. People frequently reject it and say they don't want one, or they get upset and walk out. However, in most countries, employees are entitled to a copy of the document that they sign.

The employee should get a copy of the assessment. No matter what, you should have a signed copy for the employee file. What if the employee refuses to sign? This is why you have a silent witness in the meeting with you; this silent witness can sign on the employee's behalf and always have a date with the signature, for yours the employee's and/or for the silent witness. Before you start writing people up it's important to understand how performance management works.

Defining Performance Management

There are two main parts to performance management: Behaviour and Performance. The general understanding of the performance management process is the same for either path. The paperwork and some of your wording may vary depending on what the issue is. When you performance manage someone who has a behaviour concern, the employee is breaching something from your employee handbook or the procedures and policies that employees sign upon hire. When an employee has a performance concern, this is something related to the employee's job description; it's when the employee is not performing something technical in nature or task oriented. To recap:

Performance-Based Management	Behaviour-Based Management
This is when an employee is not performing the duties on the job description, not following a company process. They are usually part of the "hard skills" of a job description / performance assessment. When a performance gap exists, it could be due to a lack of training, or an understanding of the role expectations.	These are generally the "soft skills" that are within an employee's control. They are connected to an employee's attitude, attendance, punctuality, attire, teamwork, collaboration, breach of health and safety, workplace violence harassment policies.

Examples Are:

Performance	Behaviour
Not meeting metrics, quotas, targets	Attitude, dishonesty, discourteous, disrespectful
Not completing reports	Customer service complaint, employee arguments
Failure to adhere to company standards, processes, programs	Breaking a policy, such as taking a break when not entitled to, switching a shift without permission, use of personal cell phone during work hours
Not maintaining an expected level of performance	Not complying with labour laws / health and safety laws, violating government regulations
	Failing to protect company information, conflict of interest concerns, misuse of authority, etc.

Story Time:

Human resource professionals and leaders have to prepare for a difficult or possible volatile meeting. You need to prepare the room and/or desk for safety. Remove any objects off the desk or table that could be used as a projectile. Do not sit where the employee's exit is blocked, do not be in a corner or have the employee between you and the door. If necessary, have security or police outside of the door.

Even in a meeting when you don't expect an aggressive reaction, it could happen. Always be prepared. If an employee arrives for an investigative or discipline meeting with a briefcase or backpack either have it searched by security or, at the least, ask them to place it on the floor away

*from them or across the room (unless there are security pro-
visions before entering your office).*

*Do not let the employee leave the meeting and return.
Disgruntled or terminated employees could return to the
workplace and cause harm to coworkers, management or
HR. Safety in the workplace saves lives. Workplace violence is serious and happens when you least expect it. The
actual story:*

*During a termination meeting, the employee asked for a
break in the meeting so they could retrieve their ID from
their car. The employee returned to the meeting, shot and
killed the manager and shot the assistant manager who fell
and pretended to be dead. The employee then shot himself.
This knowledge of how to prepare the environment before
an investigation or termination meeting should be first on
your list. Second, is the preparation of questions and antici-
pating the follow-up questions from responses. Thirdly, take
great notes and write down details. Review your notes
before concluding the meeting. Never make promises, do not
share names of other witnesses or other alleged violators. Be
sure the employee knows they can contact you if they have
additional information.*

Alice
40 years (Ret'd) in Employee Relations
USA

Progressive Discipline

This is the process of using a method to measure an employee's performance and course correct the performance should there be a problem.
Always remember to be fair and do not play favourites with this process

as all employees should be treated fairly. This process can be used in any environment, unionized or not. There are frequent claims within organizations and within government labour boards against leaders when employees feel they are not being treated fairly and it tends to be related to being performance managed. Generally, the progressive discipline process has three steps: Write-up # 1, Write-up # 2 and Final Write-up. However, as we discussed before, since your role as a leader is to help people succeed, it is usually recommended to have at least one step prior to jumping straight into a write-up, it can be called a counseling/coaching conversations or verbal warning.

Prior to administering performance management, please ensure your policies and processes are up to date and all employees have read, understood, and signed off on them, as well as have a copy. It is not fair to performance manage an employee when they are not aware of a policy. There will always be situations that you run into where an employee tells you/claims they don't remember a policy or procedure, which is why you get employees to sign off on all your documents and you give them a copy. It is also an employee's responsibility to read what they sign. You should remind your employees when they sign documents that they represent "their agreement" that they have read, understood, and will follow the process.

Research Steps to Progressive Discipline

Step 1: Assess the level of deficiency
There are a variety of ways to assess performance deficiency: organizational metrics, leader observation and feedback, fellow colleague and customer comments. With the latter, it is important to take the information with a grain of salt. When you see a repetition of behaviour/comments there is most likely some validity to the information you

are receiving. Sad but true, you should keep in mind that people also make complaints about others out of hatred, jealousy, or plain ignorance. Therefore, your personal observations are always most important when conducing an assessment of performance deficiency. If there is no trend and solely a one-time deficiency perhaps it will not warrant or need a full performance management process. In this case, the best course of action could be a coaching conversation and we will go into more detail a little later as what constitutes a coaching conversation. In this step, you are peeling an onion, assessing the layers of the concern to determine is it a "will" or "skill" issue. You are trying to decide if the deficiency is something within the employee's control or not.

Step 2: Determine severity

As I noted earlier, when someone is not performing there is more than a 50 per cent chance that the issue is connected to the leader. This is where you would need to reflect on your leadership skills with the individual and assess if you could have done something differently. Whether you come to this realization or not, your role is to support the employee. When assessing the severity of the deficiency you are examining the WHY and the HOW while reviewing the following items:

Obstacles: This could be a colleague that your individual does not get along with, lack of knowledge or skill. It can be a lack of training and can even be a poor company process or procedure.

Personal: Is there something going on in the individual's life that could affect their performance, create anxiety? Have you noticed a difference in your employee's behaviour? How is their health, and mental health?

Change: Have there been recent changes at work, which can affect the environment, the employee's engagement? Did the company introduce a new process, are there structural or leadership changes, which can result in lack of motivation?

Once you have completed Step 1 and 2 you will have determined if your concern is mainly a behaviour or a performance issue. Now is the time for you to do some real homework. Conducting your due diligence is not a quick and dirty task. Thoroughness is crucial as you do not want to accuse someone of something they have not done, or mildly had a part in. Investigating the concern before bringing it to the employee's attention strengthens your credibility and shows that you value your employee as you are investing time in them. Peel back all layers of that onion, assess all avenues so that you are being objective in your thinking, which can help you prepare your plan. Remember you are gathering facts, not passing judgement and prior to the next step review, go back and review your company policies, audit forms, the employee's file and any other documentation relevant to the concern so that you are well prepared.

HR Jail: A customer of mine ran into a situation once where they believed one of their employees was stealing time. The employee was leaving work early, but getting paid for it, taking longer lunches than they should and always finding a way to get paid due to excuses. Eventually, the employer peeled back the onion, gathered all the information, consulted with me and they went ahead and terminated the employee. About a few weeks later, a letter came from the Ministry of Labour for constructive dismissal. The employer asked me what to do, and I explained to them that they need to share all their evidence with the Ministry as to why they terminated the employee. The Ministry officer then shared the employer's evidence with the terminated employee to give the terminated employee a chance to reply to the evidence. The story broke down when the employee was able to prove that her employer was wrong because the camera evidence my customer was using was wrong. Due to daylight savings times and time changing twice a year, my customer never adapted the change of time on their camera systems. Which meant that all the times the employer thought the employee was leaving work early, or coming back from a lunch late was mostly not true. Therefore, the Ministry officer sided with the employee and the employer had to pay the employee termination pay. This cost the employer over $5,000 which is quite inexpensive in comparison to other situations I have seen.

Step 3: Decide your avenue of performance management

This part of this process is called progressive discipline. If an employee continues to make the same mistakes and/or has a lack of performance, your process progresses from a coaching, to a written write-up #1, written write-up # 2, etc. As the situation progresses, so does the severity of the write ups. This is why your due diligence – also known as homework – is crucial, as it allows you to determine the severity and the trend or lack thereof. For an issue to fall into the progressive discipline process, the employee must be doing the same "wrong" thing over and over even after you have coached them, and written them up. If and when an employee has a bad behaviour, or does not perform on certain tasks, yet there are no trends, this is not progressive discipline. Meaning an employee can have 10 write-ups in their file for 10 different things. Leaders tend to get upset when I share this fact with them. These 10 write-ups still constitute performance management, however not progressive discipline. The major difference is that an employee would have 10 "first written warnings" in their file thus it may be more challenging to terminate someone and prove to a government official, or even lawyer that you did everything you could to set them up for success.

Also, a termination is not supposed to be a surprise. A "first" written warning has legal terminology, which states that "should similar behaviour occur again it may result in disciplinary action up to and including termination". It is only once you get to the third and final warning that you are documenting that the employee has no more get out of jail free cards, which means one more bad move and they will be terminated. This may seem odd, and I have had leaders question me before on what the big deal is about the wording on formal write-ups, however I can confidently say the process of performance management MUST be well documented and what you say in person MUST be what is written on paper. You can provide more verbal detail, yet the legal jargon must be verbally said as its suppose to be written on paper.

The next question I tend to get is why can't a leader just jump to a final warning, especially if there are 10 different write-ups for 10 different things? The first reason you should not jump straight to a final write-up is that it is not fair, and the second reason will depend on the severity of the situation. There is a possibility of going straight to a final write-up if the concern is something quite serious, for example, an employee bullying another employee for the first time. This is severe enough to go straight to a final write up, however usually not severe enough to warrant termination. I use the word usually loosely and should this situation occur for you I would suggest you to consult your HR. Other examples could be a breach of a law such as health and safety, e.g. stepping on a shelf instead of using a ladder.

JLP TIP: Review your performance management process with your executive team to ensure all departments and leaders follow the same process. Determine on average how many chances people will be given (how many get out of jail free cards) prior to going through formal progressive discipline, e.g. can an employee be late three times before you move to the formal process?

Remember, if favouritism occurs in a business, employees will notice and when employees are upset they tend to be vocal. You should not write one employee up after they are late twice, but someone else only after three. This will affect overall morale, engagement and most importantly trust.

Performance Management Steps

A. Coaching

A coaching/counseling conversation is not a write up, it is more of an open and honest conversation, sometimes I even call it a "Get out of jail free card", taken from one of my favourite childhood games Monopoly. It is a chance to ask the employee what is going on with your behaviour, it seems you have changed, help me understand why your behaviour has changed. You would use this method if the individual has never done 'something wrong' in the past, and/ or if the situation is on a lower level of severity. During your conversation with your employee, it is important to set the context and let them know it is just a conversation. Be honest and advise them you will make a note on file such as send yourself an email to assist with remembering the date and details of the conversation. You should also clarify to the employee that this is not formal performance management.

Hopefully, you do not get blindsided. The purpose is to ask the employee their version of the situation, which should validate all the homework you previously completed. A coaching conversation can exist for many reasons. Based on your company processes, you could have several coaching conversations with someone before you move to progressive discipline. It could also be an opportunity to teach an employee something.

B. Verbal Warning

In this process, you will follow the same procedure as a coaching conversation; the main difference is this becomes the employee's first step of the progressive discipline process. As this is more formal you must advise the employee that "This is a formal verbal warning. Should similar behaviour to ABC (ABC represents the issue) occur again, it may result in further disciplinary action up to and including termination". Your method of documentation for a verbal warning is still not a formal write-up. Many leaders will send themselves an email to recap the conversation/issue as it has a date and time on it, then you can print the email and add it to the employee file. Some organizations have a record sheet where they keep track of such conversations in one location. What is important to note here is that the employee does not sign a verbal warning document as it is no longer a verbal warning when an employee signs. It is the leader who writes out the content, signs and dates the document.

JLP Tip: Every organization should have formal documents to use for performance management. It is not suggested to leave it up to a leader to create their own form. Templates and consistency are important with this process. Should the situation go sour and you need to share your documentation with a government official or lawyer in order to protect your business, accuracy is key. This is why all leaders in an organization should follow the same process.

C. Written Write-Up # 1

A regular template for a written write-up will mirror the one below. This document is usually one page in length and the words you use to describe the issue and the action you want the employee to take is important. Provide high level details without rambling; you could even use bullet points if this makes it easier for you. Always keep in mind, anything you put in writing now becomes a legal document and can be used against you.

JLP Tip: Read your document prior to having a meeting with an employee. If you feel comfortable with the document being published on the front page of a newspaper then you are good to go. If your gut tells you otherwise, then get back to the writing stage and revise your document.

Sample Written Warning

Dear Employee Name,   Date: Personal and Confidential

This shall serve as your first formal written warning concerning the incident(s) we recently discussed on XYZ date. Your (insert the appropriate word: performance / behaviour / actions) concern me and are in contradiction to (insert the appropriate sentence: tasks listed in your job description, policy in our employee handbook)

Insert Date of Verbal Warnings:

Describe the Issue: Without providing minute details, 4–8 lines describing the concern.

Remedy Required: This is where you provide suggestions for improvement. It could be additional training, job shadowing, and/or a course on anger management.

Required Date: Do not write immediately. No one including yourself can change overnight. Be respectful and provide the employee with 30–45 days to improve. Do write a specific date so the employee is clear on expectations and deadline.

Progress Report Date: This date is chosen marking halfway to your remedy required date. You want to meet and assess how the employee is doing. I.E. If you meet an employee January 5th, and their required remedy date is February 5th, the progress report date will be between January 18–21st.

Failure to achieve the required level of behaviour and performance by the pre-determined date shown above may result in further disciplinary action up to and including termination.

I look forward to continuing to support you,

Sincerely,
Please sign and date the below as acknowledgement that you have read and understood the contents of the letter as listed above.

_____   _____
Employee Signature   Date

_____   _____
Leader Signature   Date

Let's discuss a progress date in further detail: If you want to be an effective leader and be fair to your employee you should not write them up and say "see you in 30 days". You should schedule one to two progress report dates so that you have a quick conversation to recap the issue and see how the employee is doing. These meetings are also documented on a separate progress report sheet.

D. Written Write-Up # 2

This will be very similar to the written warning #1. The details of the concern may slightly vary, however the actual concern must be the same as the first to prove progressive discipline. One big difference is in the legal terminology between the first write-up and the second as listed below. You also give the employee 30–45 days to improve in this stage and also have a progress report meeting at least half way through.

This is the legal sentence that differs from the first write-up to the second write up, which should be written as the last line in the document. *This shall serve as your second formal written warning concerning the incident(s) we recently discussed*

E. Final Written Write-Up

If you get to this stage with the employee, your conversation with them should be a little sterner since this tends to be their last chance prior to you considering termination. You give the employee their last 30–45 days and set a date at the very beginning for a progress meeting half way as you did with the other two write ups. The documentation again is similar to the first and second, the different nuance is the legal terminology.

This shall serve as your third and final formal written warning concerning the incident(s) we recently discussed.

*Failure to achieve the required level of behaviour and performance by the pre-determined date shown above **will result in termination**.*

Terminations are not usually suppose to be a surprise for an employee, unless you will be paying them out (we will review this further in the chapter). When performance managing an employee and your desired result is termination, the process will take 3–6 months, therefore when you are having these open and honest conversations do not sugar coat the information. Be authentic, advise the employee they are not doing XYZ and you will support them to get them back on track. However, if they do not meet you halfway, they could be terminated. By the last and final write-up, it is important to advise the employee they will be terminated. The employee needs to know there are no more chances.

F. Progress Reports

Every time you meet with your employees, give them suggestions and directions on what they need to improve on, for each step of the process as noted above and also give them a timeline of 30–45 days. Within this 30–45 day period, you meet them at least once, if not twice, and discuss the progress of the remedy you gave them and/or they committed to. The progress report needs to be documented and added to the overall performance management documents.

Sample Progress Report

Dear Employee Name,   *Date:*   *Personal and Confidential*

This shall serve as your progress report concerning the incidents listed on the written warning report from

Insert Date of Written Warning and include a high level recap of issue:

Progress Report Date: The date you are meeting to fill out this form.

Progress Report Information: This is where you explain what progress the employee is

making, are they achieving the remedy required, if not explain why and what still needs to be done.

Next Meeting Date: Insert the date of next progress meeting, or write N/A if not applicable.

Failure to achieve the required level of behaviour and performance by the pre-determined date shown above may result in further disciplinary action up to and including termination.

I look forward to continuing to support you,

Sincerely,

Please sign and date below as acknowledgement that you have read and understood the contents of the letter as listed above.

_____   _____

Employee Signature   *Date*

_____   _____

Leader Signature   *Date*

Step 4: Performance improvement meeting

Discussions about performance or behaviour should always be in a formal setting. You do not want to have them in the lunch room or in passing so other people can hear. They should be in your office.

- » Have another leader present who is of higher status than the employee you are speaking with. If possible, a different gender to you.

- » If you can't have the employee's supervisor, then you have a neutral person like the bookkeeper. No one usually reports to the bookkeeper and the bookkeeper frequently knows when someone is being performance managed as they have access to employee files and they help you with paying people pay for their regular pay and termination pay if it's warranted.

» If you have a bookkeeper as your other witness, introduce them to the employee and advise they are just here to help take notes, not coach or mentor.

» Always have tissue and let the employee sit closest to the door.

» Set the context of the conversation based on the severity of the issue.

Story Time:

Over the years, I have had the privilege of working with many different HR professionals with varying degrees of experience and unique styles as it relates to the practice of Human Resources. Additionally, I have had many HR leaders who have provided varying leadership styles and approaches to relationship building and Employee Relations investigations.

Looking back, I really did learn from some of the best leaders who taught me both positive and negative approaches when dealing with Employee Relations situations. I would never have been equipped to deal with the situations that arise in today's workplace if it wasn't for these great lessons earlier in my HR career.

Over 12 years ago now, I was given a unique opportunity to work in an environment where people lived where they worked. Everyone worked on contract, so you could have

more than one leader during a single contract timeframe. I was new to Employee
Relations, having only worked in the Recruiting function prior to this role. This work environment was very fast-paced and could create quite a bit of stress for the employees, as their main focus was customer service. The customers were in a resort-style setting and had high expectations. The employees worked long hours for months at a time and were really not able to leave the environment that often. Additionally, the employees lived in close quarters with one another and didn't have much privacy or alone time. This environment didn't work for everyone and there were moments when individuals did not realize how different this job was until they were in the thick of it, with not many options of leaving right away.

It was in this environment where I learned a very valuable lesson regarding how to deal with individuals who are highly stressed. One of the first leaders who I worked with was the HR Manager, and he dealt with the majority of the employee relations issues that occurred. I assisted in the investigations after receiving training on how to conduct investigations. This was very valuable training that I actually use to this very day. I would often sit in when my leader was talking to employees and their leaders and quickly started to pick up on certain triggers that would either create more stress in the situation or diffuse the issue. Employees were nervous to talk to HR, so it was important to understand that and try to gauge the comfort level of the employee early in the conversation to determine the best way to move forward with the discussion. Since the goal was to get to the truth and gather information, it was important to put the employees at ease in order to gather the information and facts. I noticed that my leader, we will call him Rick, sometimes didn't read the comfort level of the employees well. I also noticed that at times, his reaction and manner tended to influence the employee and the leaders involved. The outcome to some of the cases resulted in upset leaders and/or employees who left the office feeling like the situation was not resolved. Additionally, we were not able to get all of the facts in the investigation because the employees were not comfortable enough to open up to us. I observed this and started to think about how my reaction to situations could influence the outcome for everyone involved.

Since I worked with several different leaders in this role, I was able to sit in and partner on Employee Relations situations with several other leaders. They all had different approaches and styles. Another leader, Sam, was very calm and actually had a soft approach that could diffuse the stressful situations quite quickly. My takeaway from this style was that it really worked in this particular environment. I started to use this calming approach and focused on being a good listener first, then ask questions to get the information that I needed from the employees and/or leaders. This way, we could reach the best conclusion for the situation. I was under the impression that the calming approach was good for this high stress environment, but may not be that helpful in other environments. As I have worked in different industries, I have quickly learned that all work environments can create stress and that the calming approach has helped me resolve numerous employee relations issues.

The process that I have used includes calming the individual first and actively listening to their concerns. This helps in generally trying to get the employee or leader to a better place regarding the situation.

The calming approach is not specific to the workplace, and I have found that I have used some of my calming investigative approach when dealing with friends and family. The key is to take your emotion out of the situation in order to remain unbiased and calm to assist others in calming down and sorting through the issues with them.

Geneva

19 years HR Experience

USA

Termination Meetings

As you will see, one of the repetitive things we need to do as leaders is preparation for any meeting, inclusive of termination meetings. When a situation has gotten to the point when you want to terminate the employee you should confidently be able to sleep at night because you have done everything in your power to set that employee up for success, and they have not met you halfway. This excludes if someone has done something against safety, security or against the law. Like all employee meetings, you need to prepare for your termination meeting. Part of your preparation is that you would have conducted your investigation, completed your due diligence and you need to be 100 per cent sure termination is warranted.

Contrary to what people are used to or what they may believe, there is only a 1% chance that anyone ever deserves to be terminated on the spot. Gone are the days when a leader fires someone immediately, and kicks them out of the building, that is just for the movies. Even when someone has done something serious, you still need to investigate, you still need to confirm the employee's actions by either getting them to admit what they have done or at least confirm the evidence you have with the employee directly. Even better if you get a written confession.

Like other meetings with employees, it is recommended these conversations happen in a "closed door" office setting. The employee sits closest to the door, everyone should turn off their telephones, have tissue available, have a silent witness who is someone of a different gender to you; this silent witness could also be taking notes and lastly, if possible, there should be no desk between you and the employee.

Types of Terminations

The actual terminology may vary by country and based on legislation, however in general the following descriptions will be common methods of termination:

Just Cause (also called Causal): This is when you have enough evidence to terminate someone without giving them notice in writing and/or you are not paying them out. Possible reasons could be: your employee has stolen something from the business, they have drastically broken your company policies, the employee has done something against safety, security, or against the law. If there is a performance concern, you most likely have gone through formal performance management and have a minimum of three write-ups as you have conducted progressive discipline. Let's also keep in mind that you could have jumped to a final warning depending on the severity of the issue. You are not choosing termination as there is a reoccurring issue after the final write up.

Without Cause: As the words explain you do not have a justifiable reason to terminate because without cause means no reason. When you do not have enough reason to terminate someone yet you want them out of the business you will need to consult your legislation to determine how much written notice or pay in lieu of notice you need to provide, plus you have to consider severance or common law pay as well. If you do not follow your legislation during a termination, you could be creating risk for your business to get sued, fined, or undergo a Ministry investigation. Without cause terminations do not tend to be cheap, therefore this method is not usually recommended unless your paperwork is very strong as you conducted a thorough performance management process.

Under probation: Many provinces and countries have different legislation with respect to probation. It can also depend on your profession. As we have noted before, most are anywhere between 30 days, 90 days and six months. Before you consider this type of termination you need to review your laws. Then, what type of probationary assessment do you have? Your organization should have a document for leaders to use that measures some basic soft and hard skills to determine if you want to keep the employee past the probation period. The challenge with assessing someone during this period is that an employee could be on their best behaviour because they want to pass the probationary period. It's called the honeymoon phase. If you have any indication that the employee may not be a right fit for you, follow your gut and investigate. As soon as you pass your legislative probation you fall into a whole different set of laws that will most likely make it difficult, and more costly, for you to terminate.

Working Notice: When you want to get rid of someone who is not performing, yet perhaps they are not a threat to the business so you are "okay" with having them work for several more weeks before their last day. For the employee this may be hard and unless the working notice is mutual, an employee will be upset they are expected to work yet know they are being terminated soon. Some will no longer show up for work, but this does not mean as the employer you can change the termination date. If you provided notice, you are providing one week per year of service or as deemed appropriate according to your laws. When someone chooses to not fulfill their notice period, you still need to keep them on payroll, allow them to have the benefits you were already providing and terminate them on the date when the notice period expires. As the employer, if you change this, you are no longer providing working notice and therefore changing the terms and conditions of your notice to a termination without cause and open up your cheque book. I personally only recommend working notice for a short period of time, two weeks or less. I can't see how any employee including if it was myself being advised by my boss, "Thanks for your efforts; we don't need you anymore; but can you still work your shifts for the next few weeks." I would want to bail like any other person unless you were really strapped for money.

Sometimes, you can combine working notice with termination pay if perhaps there is a large restructuring happening, a business is closing, or you have a situation that is not cut and dried and perhaps you want to go above and beyond the law.

Pay In Lieu of Notice: This is when you are looking to get rid of someone now and you no longer want them in your business, you also do not need a reason. Pay in lieu of notice is part of Without Cause, hence why you do not need a reason. Based on your legislation, you tend to pay one week per year of service up to a certain number of weeks. Once your employee's tenure passes this "certain number of weeks" you get into different laws, which means more money. Therefore, taking this route is usually only suggested for someone that is low tenured.

Frustration of Contract: This is not a common type of termination and may or may not exist based on your legislation. After someone has been away from the business for a lengthy period of time, usually several years and there is no chance that the employee will be returning to work in the foreseeable future, you may determine to frustrate the contract. It is almost like you are not really terminating them because if they were willing or had come back to work they would have been working. The employee also did not resign, yet as the employer, you have decided you are no longer keeping their job for them. You usually have to pay the statutory minimums that your legislation requires and your termination letter would differ slightly to others.

Job Abandonment: When an employee has not shown up for several consecutive shifts in a row you may be able to assume they are never coming back. In many jurisdictions, this happens after three consecutive shifts in a row, yet check your law to be sure. A few steps that are important is to give an employee the benefit of the doubt before assuming they are not returning to work. Send the employee a letter via registered mail asking them where they are, because they are MIA – missing in action. Give them five business days to get back to you and write this in the letter. Be clear you want to hear from them by Friday 5:00 p.m. Why registered mail? Because you want the proof they got the message. You can track registered letters on your local postal service website. If the employee does not pick up the registered letter you can just keep it in the employee file and wait another five business days or so before sending a job abandonment letter.

Story Time:

I worked with a client for several years and one day he called me to say one of his employees had not shown up for work for several days. He tried to call the employee's home, cell phone, left messages and even sent emails. He was a bit nervous as it was not typical behaviour so he even called the employee's emergency contacts. The client and I kept in close contact as he was upset. He could not believe this employee was doing this to him, especially at this time of year. It was year-end for this company and the employee who had not shown up was responsible for a big report that gets released to the whole company. The next step that I suggested was a registered letter asking where is the employee and asking for her to get in contact with him by a specific date and time. He sent this MIA letter, gave the employee the usual five business days to get back and still when he did not hear back he waited another several weeks before removing the employee from payroll and issuing a record of employment. He was so upset, he was actually hurt that this person whom be believed was a good employee just up and left him without any notice and was nowhere to be found. About six weeks later the client called me frantically upset and almost crying. His employee who went MIA just called him, she was in the hospital from a car accident and was hurt pretty badly. She had undergone several surgeries and still needed more. My client's emotions were like a roller coaster. One minute he was crying, the next mad at himself for thinking so negatively of her when she didn't show up. Luckily, the employee recovered well and was eventually able to return to work months later. This client and I still talk, and I use his story frequently as an example that it is human nature to jump to conclusions, assuming something negative and judge. It's ok, his thinking was not malicious just from force of habit. Showing us we all have opportunities with trying to assume positive intent instead of negative.

Termination Checklist

What To Do	What Not To Do
Terminate at the beginning of a shift	Do not terminate at the end of a shift, it's rude as you have known the whole shift you were going to terminate and you used them for the shift
Review your legislation to see how many hours you need to pay the employee for the termination meeting. It varies from three hours to the whole shift.	Do not terminate over the phone, or text message, or social media or even by email. Only and only if someone does not show up for work can you terminate with a registered letter
Terminate in person	Do not terminate on a weekend and preferably not a Friday afternoon as your Ministry of labour closes, and it does not give the employee enough time to contact them or exercise their rights
Always have two leaders present of opposite gender and of higher status than the employee	Do not terminate on a public holiday, birthday, religious day
Have the meeting in an office, not in a glass room where everyone can see. If you have a glass door in your office you should have some sort of curtain	Do not walk the employee out of the building –that is humiliating. You have just fired them that is hard enough to take. Exception: If the employee stole from you and/or is causing a scene then you can walk them out
Give them time to gather their things	Do not rush the employee
Allow the employee to still come to your business if they want, (they probably won't) however if you are a grocery store for example, your former employee is still a customer	Only ban or trespass an employee if absolutely necessary
Ask for their keys, passcodes, uniforms, etc. during the meeting. Usually even have them sign a document that they will return all company property by a specific date.	Do not hassle the employee. If they do not give you the company property after a few requests, move on. It is a bigger argument that will waste your time to pursue than to walk away peacefully

What To Do	What Not To Do
Always have a termination letter that you have prepared in advance and provided in person	Do not mail the termination letter to an employee unless it is your absolute last resort. These letters should be given in person
Close up the employee file in an efficient time frame. Issue a record of employment, remove them from the system, etc.	The longer you wait to change their status in the system (e.g. from employee to customer, or removing them from the employee list) this could be used against you as there are laws as to when some of these requirements must be done
Send yourself an email on how the termination meeting went. Keep verbatim notes in case you get sued; you may need them. Ask your silent witness (other leader) to send you an email with their version of how the meeting went, who said what, etc.	Do not write these notes in a note-book as there are no dates or times outside of what you hand write. If you have no other choice okay, however you can write out the whole notebook the day before you have to hand over evidence to a lawyer for example. Meaning, it's best to have something that is date and time stamped
Speak to the highest level of leaders after a termination meeting to advise them of the change and have them help you manage the situation and reduce gossip. Then those leaders can discuss with their direct reports and so on	Do not let people hear about it through the grapevine. Always put an immediate stop to any gossip
You can issue the last paycheque by cheque instead of direct deposit to have the employee pick up the cheque as it's an opportunity for them to return company property	Do not terminate in public, on the spot or engage on in a lengthy debate
You should pay out any commissions, allowances the employee would normally be entitled to	If you terminate someone before they are to receive a major commission cheque it is rude to not pay this out. (Unless the employee has stolen or done something against the law)

Exit Interviewing:

It is not as popular as other HR practices, however I do recommend it as an opportunity to talk to your employee before they leave your business. Over the years of conducting exit interviews, people have really opened up, shared information about your business, culture and fellow employees that could possibly amaze you. People feel more comfortable being honest with you because they will never see you again. If they want, they can even delete you from Facebook. The format for this meeting does not need to be as formal as other meetings, and it's important to plan as you would other meetings. It can take 15–20 minutes or longer if you would prefer. Some suggested questions are:

» What did you think of our orientation and training programs?
» Why did you start looking for a new job?
» Did you feel you had the tools and success you needed to do your job?
» How would you describe the culture in our company?
» Did you feel you were respected at our company?
» What could I have done to keep you here?
» What did you find most satisfying about your role?
» Did you share your concerns with anyone prior to looking for a new job?
» If you could change one thing about your job, what would it be?
» How did you find the management team at our business, did you feel comfortable bringing your concerns to them?
» Did you receive constructive feedback to help with your performance?
» Is there anything additional you would like to add?

As you have done with other areas of HR, create a template that you can use and also for all your leadership team to ensure consistency within the business.

Story Time:

During an exit interview I did over 10 years ago, I became exposed to a variety of reasons why these meetings are so important. I have never forgotten and frequently use this one as an example thus I wanted to share the story with you. I was working with 950 employees on a cruise line, and the employee I was interviewing was a supervisor in the restaurant department. Usually, the restaurant manager would do the exit interview but for this particular employee he advised us he was resigning because he had a better opportunity back in his country. Naturally, I would want not to be skeptical of someone's reasons for leaving a job, yet something just didn't feel right. I therefore offered to the restaurant manager to complete the exit interview.

We had our meeting the day before he was leaving the ship. We started the meeting at 9:00 a.m. and it ended just after 11:00 a.m. I had to call the restaurant manager to let him know he was going to be late. We will call him James. James was shy at the beginning so I started by asking him the basic questions similar to what is listed above from a template I had created. About 15 minutes into our conversation I said to him, "You are giving me all the answers you think I want to hear, however this is not the purpose of an exit interview. James, I am genuinely interested in why you are leaving a job where you have been for over 10 years, making very good money, you are able to provide for your family and with almost no notice you are deciding to leave."

James got a little emotional, he seemed embarrassed that he had tears in his eyes. He proceeded to tell me that the restaurant manager was verbally abusive, he has been for several contracts. To clarify, a contract could last 6–8 months, which meant this restaurant manager was verbally abusive for years. Then James continued to explain that he was quite sure the restaurant manager was stealing money from the company and sharing it amongst some of his favourites. I asked James "I assume you are not one of the favourites?" He said, "No. I am. I've gotten a lot of extra money over the past few years, it has tormented me. I can't do it anymore, and I am prepared to give it back."

My reply to James was the following: Making claims of harassment and stealing are strong allegations and are you sure, 100 per cent sure you stand by what you are saying?" James replied, "Yes." I said, "Okay."

Then our conversation turned down a different avenue, and we started talking about facts, dates and as many details as I could obtain from him, as he was leaving the ship the next day. Why this story is so powerful is that it took a long-term employee's integrity to be questioned over and over and over and although he was benefiting from it, it was really helping his family, and extended family, he felt bullied, mentally exhausted from all the lies, and could not handle it anymore.

Every exit interview is not going to be a gold mine, yet you never know if you don't ask. To ensure your department and organization is fair and equitable it is always recommended to have consistency with all leaders. If you will take on the practice of exit interviewing, all employees should be given this opportunity in person or if this is not possible to create a questionnaire to send online.

Performance Management Takeaways

A leader's role is to set employees up for success. Performance management is a tool for development and should not be seen as a process to fire

✓ Conduct performance assessments (if possible 1x per quarter otherwise 2x per year). Gone are the days of conducting a performance review once a year

✓ Understand the difference between the types of performance management so that you use them appropriately to help development your employee

✓ Always document your performance conversations in formal letters or through email as you never know when you will need the information

✓ No matter what the situation, everyone deserves to be treated with respect and dignity

Final Thoughts

———

Remember! Your employees are also your customers and ambassadors to your brand."

———

Being a leader is a big responsibility, one that you need to be ready to fulfill. It is common nowadays to end up in a leadership position before you might be quite ready or even having been in a leadership role for years and all of a sudden start experiencing "HR issues". Do not worry, 99 per cent of the things you encounter in HR you can handle. The type of leader you want to be is completely your choice. If you seek a happy engaging workplace then you need to be a happy and engaged leader. You need to feel confident, be confident and have a good foundation on what it means to lead people.

Use this book as a constant guide and not just to read once then place on the shelf. Think of it as your 24/7 HR consultant who can coach you on different facets of human resources whenever you need it day or night. As a leader and business owner, it is important to remember that your employees are also your customers and ambassadors to your brand. Treating them well will not only benefit them it will benefit you, your business and your external customer.

Whether you are just starting out, you are a newly-promoted leader and/or a seasoned leader, we are all in the business of customer service; be it our internal or external customer. We can all use tips, tricks and extra tools for our belt that can give us a different perspective on how to provide exemplary customer service. Within all my years in this profession, I can certainly attest to no two situations being the same. Nothing is black and white; it's just a crap load of grey. There are frequent similarities between situations and concerns, and once you have experienced something once or twice you will feel more confident on how to handle it the third and fourth time. Yet, we all know that people are different and nine times out of 10 people bring a different twist on a situation as we are unique human beings. It's another reason why understanding HR is important for any leader.

Understanding HR is not just about performance reviews, and writing people up. You should no longer feel anxious or get exhausted dealing with "HR issues" in the workplace. Do not focus on what you can't control and only what you can. Your leadership and how you handle situations is what you can control. When you are unsure of something, and your batteries are low, pick up this book, read the chapter that pertains to your questions /concerns and it will help you recharge and get back on track.

The book is not to be considered legal advice, yet an opportunity to learn and keep things simple by instantly applying what you learn. Always remember to help each other, use other fellow leaders as thinking partners as well as your HR consultant.

Thank you for taking the time to read this book, and I sincerely hope the contents will be helpful to you and your journey as a leader. Perhaps we will cross paths and you will be willing to share your story of how this book has helped you.

You are now ready to create a stronger workplace by incorporating these practices, and remember to always ask WHY, make your own interpretation on things and stay out of HR Jail ☺